Tales of a ...
TEA LEAF

The Complete Guide to Tea Cuisine

JILL YATES

SQUAREONE
PUBLISHERS

COVER DESIGNER: Jacqueline Michelus
TYPESETTER: Gary A. Rosenberg • EDITOR: Elaine Weiser

The quote on page 13 is reprinted from the article *"Tea Readings Span the Globe"*
written by Diana Rosen, courtesy of www.sallys-place.com.

The quotes on pages 20 and 23 are reprinted from *The Evolution of American Tea Culture*
by Tomislav Podreka and appear courtesy of *Fresh Cup Magazine's Tea Almanac 2001.*
Tomislav Podreka is the owner of Serendipitea, a tea company specializing in fine teas.

The quote on page 94 is reprinted courtesy of the Oregon State News & Communications Services,
Linus Pauling Institute, Oregon State University.

Square One Publishers • 115 Herricks Road • Garden City Park, NY 11040
(516) 535-2010 • (877) 900-BOOK • www.squareonepublishers.com

Library of Congress Cataloging-in-Publication Data

Yates, Jill.
    Tales of a tea leaf / Jill Yates.
        p. cm.
    Includes bibliographical references and index.
    ISBN 0-7570-0099-1
    1. Cookery (Tea) 2. Tea. I. Title.

TX817.T3Y38 2005
641.6'372—dc22

                                                    2005002185

Printed in the United States of America

10   9   8   7   6   5   4   3   2   1

Contents

To Gregory, always

Preface

As much as I enjoy, crave, and even depend on my morning cup of tea to warm and wake me with its precious dose of caffeine, I admit I was a creature of convenience. My cupboard, though stocked with colorful stacks of boxed tea bags, did not contain any loose leaf tea.

I could blame my childhood, as I was never taught the pleasures of tea. While my mother's family tree does have a few Irish and British branches, the typical cultural appreciation for tea was not passed on through the generations. I was raised in a solid coffee-craving family—the kind where the three-pound can of ground coffee was as much a staple in the pantry as milk and eggs in the refrigerator. My folks brewed their coffee in a percolator, a shiny, streamlined machine that purred and churned with a rhythmic hum, its beloved brew bubbling through the pot top's clear cap. I found it curious that a seemingly simple device transformed what looked like coarse brown sand into a steaming, rich liquid. I enjoyed the aroma, but never acquired a taste for its bold brew. However, I found consuming coffee in a delicious treat like a batch of brownies or a slice of tiramisu is a wonderful way to enjoy its rich flavor. Even marrying a devout coffee consumer did not persuade me. Despite overwhelming influences to the contrary, I remain true to tea.

It was years later that I began thinking outside the bargain box of tea. But from my first steaming cup of Hairy Crab Oolong, I was hooked. And with my newfound enthusiasm came curiosity. Once I began looking into the story of tea, I was fascinated. It was this fascination that led to the book you're holding in your hands. But it would not have been possible without the assistance of many people who helped me along the way.

Many thanks to Rudy Shur and his staff at Square One Publishers, especially editor Elaine Weiser, and to the individuals and organizations whose contribution of recipes made this book possible. A list of contributors is included in the Permission Credits section, beginning on page 177. Special thanks also go to the Tea Associations of the United States, Canada, and the United Kingdom for their assistance. Warm appreciation goes to my friend Rosanne Susan Ponchick for her enthusiasm for tea and this book. Sincere thanks to my friends Mona Ail and Tomi Mosby, who cheered me on, kept me laughing, and were always on the lookout for tea information. And I am especially grateful to my husband, Gregory, who is my constant source of encouragement, my editor, and the one who, by example, always challenges me to do my best.

Introduction

What exactly is tea? Much more than a drink, tea is a story. A story that captivates—if only for the fact that such an unassuming bush produces simple green leaves that are the source of the world's oldest and most popular beverage. Over a trillion cups of tea are consumed throughout the world every year. But the story of tea is much more than a mere curiosity. It is an incredible tale of royals and rebels, of ingenuity and intrigue, power and perseverance. It is a story where millionaires are made and murders plotted. Infused with mystery, the story of tea is steeped in history and has been brewing for nearly 5,000 years.

There are "real" teas—black, green, oolong, and white—made from the *Camellia sinensis* plant that can be blended, scented, and flavored; herbal teas, which aren't "real" tea; terrific teas like chai, kombucha, and bubble tea; and special teas like yerba mate, kava, and rooibos. Clearly, this tea party is not just for your grandmother anymore. Tea's hip and healthful image has spawned a new generation of teetotalers who seek out and can afford the very best. But the good news is that even rare teas are affordable.

In "The Life and Times of the Tea Leaf," Part One of *Tales of a Tea Leaf*, we'll explore the centuries' old lore and lure of tea. In Chapter 1, we will take a look at the legends of the leaf, which include a Chinese emperor and an Indian monk. We'll follow tea's journey to the West and learn about the revered author who changed the way the world looks at tea.

In Chapter 2, we'll see how the business of tea has shaped history. From England's not-so-honorable Honorable East India Company to tea caravans and clipper ships, the tea trade has been spiced with smugglers, rascals, and determined entrepreneurs, some who have become household names.

What's the difference between green tea and black tea, and how should each be brewed? With so many varieties of tea, it can be confusing. In Chapter 3, we'll consider some basics of tea, including tea types, herbals, and how to brew the perfect cup of tea.

Where in the world does tea come from? In Chapter 4, we'll plot a course of discovery and follow the trail of tea to distant lands where we'll learn where in the world tea grows and what it takes to cultivate a cup of tea.

In Chapter 5, we'll peek into the world of medical research where recent studies have propelled tea into the headlines. There have been astonishing reports linking tea drinking from everything to cutting cavities and curing cancer to impeding heart disease and strokes. Is the miracle of tea myth or science? You may be surprised at the answer.

In Part Two, "The Tastes and Pleasures of the Tea Leaf," the fun really begins. We get to eat, drink, and be merry. Roll up your sleeves, invite some friends over, and get cooking. Chapter 6 and Chapter 7 bring together recipes for hot and cold drinks—some even with alcohol (that's where the merry part comes in), side dishes, main meals, and desserts—all made with tea. *Mexican Tea Punch, Austrian Peach Cookies, Pumpkin Chai Pie,* and *Tea Smoked Chicken* are only a sampling of the exotic tastes that await your exploration.

Do you like trivia, odd bits of history, quotes, and a good story? You'll find those here too, so you can please your palate and satisfy your curiosity at the same time. For example, did you know there was a plot to kill Hitler with a cup of tea? Did you know tea played a role in the attempt to remove impeached President Andrew Johnson from office? Have you heard about the Tea Lady from Teaneck, New Jersey, who taught her students the value of a million by having them collect tea tags from around the world. In the process, they stirred up some national attention and created their own brand of tea. Read on.

There are nearly 3,000 varieties of tea and even more stories to tell, so with *Tales of a Tea Leaf,* we will just begin our exploration, but it's a great way to become familiar with, and ultimately savor, the lore. So settle down with a good cuppa and enjoy the tea-riffic journey. I'll have another cup myself—milk, no sugar please.

Why not consecrate ourselves to the queen of the Camellias,
and revel in the warm stream of sympathy that flows from her altar?
In the liquid amber within the ivory porcelain,
the initiated may touch the sweet reticence of Confucius,
the piquancy of Lao Tzu,
and the ethereal aroma of Sakyamuni himself.

—KAKUZO OKAKURA (1862–1913)
THE BOOK OF TEA

PART ONE

The**Life**&**Times**of the**TeaLeaf**

CHAPTER 1

Inthe**Beginning**

Where there's tea there's hope.

—SIR ARTHUR PINERO
(1855–1934), BRITISH AUTHOR

S o how did it all begin, this tale of the tea leaf? Tea's elusive past is steeped in stories, legends really, from the Far East where the stirring liquor of the leaves has seeped into the very fabric of society and created a culture that culminates in a cup. Often told, the rich accountings of emperors, spiritual leaders, kings, and queens represent the allure and lore that has accompanied tea, the world's most consumed beverage next to water, for nearly 5,000 years.

There are nearly 3,000 varieties of tea, but only one plant. Black, green, oolong, and white tea all come from the *Camellia sinensis* leaf, a white-flowering evergreen shrub originally found in China, Tibet, and northern India. Whether you prefer a flavorful Darjeeling from the foothills of the Himalayas, a smoky Chinese Lapsang Souchong, or rich, sweet Indian Chai, it is the cultivation and manufacture of this legendary leaf that results in your favorite type of tea (a subject explored in Chapters 3 and 4).

ANCIENT TEA TALES

In the beginning, it is said the pleasure of drinking tea was discovered in 2737 BCE. The legend is credited to the famous Chinese Emperor Shen Nong, acclaimed as the "Father of Chinese Medicine." As the story unfolds, Shen Nong is sitting by an open fire about to refresh himself with a cup of boiling water. Some say he was in his garden, others say he was traveling away from home, but most agree he was ahead of his time by recognizing the benefit of boiling water before drinking it. Leaves from a nearby bush blew into his kettle and he found the resulting brew soothing and pleasing to taste. Some attribute authorship of the ancient medical book, the *Pen Ts'ao,* to Shen Nong, in which tea is noted for its pleasurable and medicinal qualities, as it "gives one vigor of body, contentment of mind, and determination of purpose, when taken over a long period of time."

Taoists describe tea as an "indispensable ingredient in the elixir of immortality."

The much revered Japanese tea ceremony is linked to another story of tea's discovery. Bodhidharma, or Daruma as he is called in Japan, was a missionary Buddhist monk who traveled from his native India to China at the end of the fifth century. Upon arrival in the Far East, he is credited with founding the Zen school of Buddhism, known as *Ch'an* in China.

Zen teaches that through divine meditation supreme self-realization can be attained, and Bodhidharma's dedication to meditation is legendary. One story claims he meditated so long with his legs folded, he lost circulation and his legs fell off. But the most famous tale is told that in 520 CE he was determined to meditate in front of a wall for a period of nine years. After several years passed, fatigue overwhelmed him and he fell asleep. Bodhidharma was so troubled by his failure of allowing sleep to interfere with his meditation that he cut off the offending body parts—his eyelids. Where the eyelids fell, tea plants grew, thereby providing a refreshing and stimulating beverage used by worshipers to stay alert for centuries. In the highly esteemed *The Book of Tea*, author Kakuzo Okakura explains that later, Buddhist monks in Japan "gathering before his image drank tea out of a single bowl with profound formality of a holy sacrament. It was this Zen ritual which finally developed into the Tea Ceremony of Japan in the fifteenth century."

Legends are, well, legendary and inherently difficult to dispel, as each telling reinforces their place in history. But regarding the origin of tea, we do know the *Camellia sinensis* plant (from which all tea is derived) is native to China where, before it was cultivated to perfection, it grew wild on the mountainsides and in the valleys. So it is possible to imagine a leaf landing in Shen Nong's pot, bringing forth the pleasures of tea for all creation.

EARLY RECORDS OF TEA

If we look to literature to answer the question of how the tale of tea began, it's about as clear as a fine cup of Darjeeling with just a bit of cream. Some scholars think its first mention could have been in the Chinese *Book of Songs*, written no later than the sixth century BCE. The Chinese character *t'u* appears throughout the book, and at that time it is believed one of the meanings for *t'u* was tea. Also, *t'u*, except for one stroke, is the same character for *ch'a*, which means tea today. The change from using the character *ch'a* in place of *t'u* appeared early in the Han Dynasty (206 BCE to 220 CE). Because *t'u* was also used for other plants like sow thistle, it's a change that could have signaled tea's growing importance, requiring its own character.

Lu Yu, "God of Tea"

What is absolutely clear is that the Chinese poet, Lu Yu, changed the world's perception of tea and brought the process and pleasure of drinking tea to a national boil. He was born in the eighth century CE at a time when tea drinking was wide-

The author Okakura describes the Philosophy of Tea, or Teaism, as the Art of Life, a religion of aestheticism covering "our whole point of view about man and nature." It is the very measure of a man, where a man with "no tea" in him is considered insensitive and a man described with "too much tea" in him is too sensitive.

spread, but people knew little about it. Tea merchants hired Lu Yu to write a practical guide for tea. It took him five years, but his three-part magnum opus *Ch'a Ching,* or *The Classic of Tea,* achieved a poetry of prose that had a profound effect on Eastern culture and remains in print today, over 1,200 years later. It was the first work to document, instruct, and describe the full cycle of tea from planting the seeds to pouring it from the pot. An orphan raised by Buddhist monks, Lu Yu left the monastery as an adult, but wrote of tea with a reverence for the subject and appreciation for the ceremony often attributed to his spiritual training.

The first part of Lu Yu's book discusses tea's beginnings and its manufacture. The second part educates the reader on the necessary "equipage" of tea, which uses not less than twenty-four tools that are required to prepare and brew tea:

> However, when in the walled city at the gate of a Prince or Duke, if the twenty-four implements find their number diminished by only, then it is best to dispense with the tea.

In the third part, Lu Yu describes how to brew and drink tea, instructing his readers on the importance of moderation, "the very essence of tea," saying, "for exquisite freshness and vibrant fragrance, limit the number of cups to three. If one can be satisfied with less than perfection, five are permissible."

The publication of *The Classic of Tea* made Lu Yu a cultural icon. He was befriended by the emperor, revered by the people, and sacrifices were offered up to him as the god of tea. His work elevated tea to an art form associated with every aspect of Eastern existence. In fact, Taoists—followers of a Chinese philosophy originating in the sixth century BCE advocating simplicity and selflessness— describe tea as an "indispensable ingredient in the elixir of immortality."

Tea Arrives In Japan

Buddhist monks returning from study in China brought tea back to Japan as early as the eighth century. In 729 CE the Japanese Emperor Shomu is reported to have invited 100 Buddhist monks to his palace for tea. And when Buddhist monk Eisai

"There are many ways to put into practice in our lives the teaching of the great masters of the past. In Zen, truth is pursued through the discipline of meditation in order to realize enlightenment, while in Tea we use training in the actual procedures of making tea to achieve the same end."

—Sen no Rikyu, Japanese Tea Master

returned from China in 1191 as a Zen master, he not only brought to Japan the new school of Buddhism, but also new tea seeds and the powdered form of tea (matcha) used in the Japanese tea ceremony. Eisai touted tea's spiritual, stimulating, and healing properties and later wrote Japan's first book on tea, *Kissa Yojok* (*The Book of Tea Sanitation*). Ceremonial teas remained in Japan's temples and lavish social teas remained in the grand parlors of the upper classes until Zen priest and tea master Murata Juko (Shuko) broke tradition by creating the beloved tea ceremony, which was adopted by the entire country.

JAPANESE TEA CEREMONY

The Japanese tea ceremony is *chanoyu*, which literally means "hot water for tea." Zen priest Murata Juko (1422–1502) is considered the father of the Japanese tea ceremony, as he combined the ritual preparation, service, and drinking of tea with a spiritual sense of humility and tranquility inspired by his Zen training. The resulting *chado*, or the Way of Tea, transformed the act of drinking tea into a sacred discipline. Juko moved the tea ceremony out of the majestic parlors and

The elegant Japanese tea ceremony, c. 1900.

into an intimate, unadorned setting, thereby emphasizing the importance of inner wealth over outward riches. Seeking the essence of *wabi*, an important concept of Japanese aesthetics that includes elements of serenity and austerity, Juko created a tea ceremony with refined simplicity in which all participants are given equal respect—regardless of their social status. While tea master Takeno Joo (1502–1555) later expanded upon Juko's innovation by refining the wabi aesthetics of the ceremony, Joo is most noted for having taught his famous disciple, Sen no Rikyu.

Sen no Rikyu, Grand Tea Master

Sen no Rikyu (1522–1591) was the greatest of all tea masters. Through a proficiency many practitioners would insist requires a lifetime to master, he refined

*Ah, how wonderful
that tea, plucked ere
the kindly breeze

Had swept away
the pearling frost
upon its leaves

And the tiny leaf-
buds shone like gold!

Being packed
when fresh and
redolent of firing,

Its essential goodness
had been cherished,
instead of wasted.

Such tea was
intended for the court
and high nobility;

How had it reached
the hut of a humble
mountain-dweller?*

—Lu Tung, c. Eighth
Century, Chinese Poet

the tea ceremony to its highest state of perfection. Guided by the four principles of harmony, respect, purity, and tranquility, the spirit of Rikyu's tea ceremony teaches enlightenment through disciplined training in the tea ritual. In designing the first separate "teahouse," Rikyu used these principles to celebrate harmony with man and nature.

For example, the teahouse, a small, humble building, holds the tearoom, a place where every object has a purpose, no color or design is repeated, and no movement is wasted. The garden path that leads to the teahouse is a symbol of the path to enlightenment; the walk through the garden emphasizes man's unity with nature. The requirement that guests must then crawl through a small entrance door encourages humility and eliminates social status.

The great-grandson of Rikyu, Senso Soshitsu, practiced a tea ritual that developed into the Urasenke tradition of tea. The fourteenth-generation descendent of Rikyu, Grand Master Tantansai (Sekiso Soshitsu), established the Urasenke Foundation in 1949. It has since become one of the most popular traditions of tea in Japan and around the world. Sen Soshitsu XVI, the sixteenth-generation descendent of Sen no Rikyu, continues the practice of his ancestors as the grand tea master. He succeeded his father, Sen Soshitsu XV, in December 2002.

THE TEA LEAF TRAVELS WEST

During Sen no Rikyu's lifetime, word of the East's devotion to tea reached Europe. The first mention of tea in the Western world was published in 1559 in Venice—the sixteenth-century center of trade between East and West. Referring to the numerous health benefits of *Chai Catai* (tea of China), Giambattista Ramusio, in Volume II of *Navigatione et Viaggi,* quotes the merchant Hajji Mohammed as saying "those people would gladly give a sack of rhubarb for one ounce of Chai Catai."

In 1597 tea is first mentioned in English, translated from the journal writings of Dutch navigator Jan Hugo van Lin-Schooten, who traveled to the East while sailing for the Portuguese. His enthusiastic reporting on the Japanese tea rituals, cherished utensils, and other items of wealth was the impetus for the Dutch to send merchant ships to the island of Java in Indonesia, where they set up head-quarters for Asian trade.

About the time van Lin-Schooten was recording his observations on the importance of tea in Japanese culture, Catholic missionaries were working to bring the message of the Church to the Chinese. The Church's earlier success in China was wiped out when the Ming Dynasty took control in 1368. By the late 1500s, all the Catholic missions had disappeared and the Church had to start all over again.

The Chinese, distrustful of the European traders, restricted them to the trading ports in southern China. Catholic missionaries, however, were gradually allowed access inland where they developed closer relationships with the Chinese, learning about their customs, culture, and esteem for tea. Of the several missionaries who mentioned tea in their writings, Father Matteo Ricci was the most well known.

In his letters, Father Ricci credits the Chinese appreciation for tea to long life and good health. One can imagine the good Father sipping a cup of fine Chinese tea when he wrote the *T'ien-chu-she-i* (*True Doctrine of God*), which explains the essential doctrines of the faith and arguments of reason culled from Chinese writings and Christian philosophy and theology. Called "the manual of the missionaries," it brought respect and many converts to the Catholic faith in China and other Asian countries.

While the Catholic Church looked upon China and its people as a vast land of pagans to proselytize, much of the Western world was beating a path to its doorstep. But those Westerners did not want to aid in the salvation of souls; rather, they merely desired to reap profits from trading in Chinese silks, pottery, porcelain—and especially tea.

The Dutch Bring Tea to Europe

In 1602, the States-General of the Netherlands incorporated a collection of small

"The first time I was a guest at a Urasenke Foundation tea class to observe chanoyu, the Japanese tea ceremony, I came away with an aura of serenity around me that lasted for weeks. Chanoyu is the cultivated pursuit of tea; the art of tea. The precision, the discipline, the exactness of teacher and student were all-encompassing. As an observer, I felt like a part of the audience at an exquisite ballet."

—Diana Rosen, *"Tea Readings Span the Globe"*

Father Matteo Ricci

A lover of tea, Jesuit priest, and native of Rome, Father Ricci lived in China from 1582 until his death in 1610. Considered the founder of China's Catholic missions, his methods brought great success and controversy to the Catholic Church in China. Using advancements in mathematics, science, and the arts, Father Ricci appealed to the Chinese intellect and inspired curiosity in the faith. He also exercised tolerance for Chinese rites and rituals used to honor ancestors as well as Confucius, believing they were a national tradition of honor and respect, not religious worship. Some Jesuits and many more priests from Franciscan and Dominican orders disagreed, certain these practices weakened the faith. The disagreement continued for nearly a century after Father Ricci's death, until the pope finally settled the matter in 1704, deciding against the tolerance of rites.

"There is not alone a single quality of excellence in the leaf, for one surpasses the other."

—Father Matteo Ricci

trading companies to exact control over the Asian trade. They were given government powers to maintain and engage military force, enact justice, coin money, and establish treaties. The group was called *Verenigde Oostindische Compagnie* (United East India Company), now known as the Dutch East India Company, or the VOC. It was a Dutch company merchant ship that brought the first tea from China and Japan to Europe in 1610. Tea's popularity grew slowly, as it was very expensive and originally looked upon as an exotic specialty drink for the rich. Tea was often served at high society tea parties in Holland where guests gorged themselves on sweet cakes, tobacco, and as much as fifty or more cups of tea.

The Dutch company was in business for nearly 200 years, with headquarters in the city of Batavia (Jakarta), Indonesia. In 1652, it also established Cape Colony on Table Bay, the first European settlement in South Africa located near present-day Cape Town. In 1669, at the peak of its power, the Dutch company had forty warships, 150 merchant ships, and 10,000 soldiers. The Dutch required such a force to keep up with its fiercest competitor, the English East India Company (see Chapter 2).

Tea Time for England

During the middle of the seventeenth century, tea was introduced in England, where it was received like a stray dog. The noble leaf was first admitted with hesitation, but gradually England's fondness for tea grew to the point where life couldn't be imagined without its warm and cheering influence. To the rest of the world, Britain's bond with tea is forever linked to its identity.

In 1657, the first establishment to sell tea in England was Thomas Garway's Coffeehouse in London. Twenty-two years later on March 11, 1679, the English East India Company began a long tradition of public tea auctions in London. London, once a critical center for the international tea trade, received shipments of tea leaves from around the world, packed in 100-pound wooden chests. Technology put an end to 319 years of tradition on June 29, 1998, when the final London tea auction was held. What once had lasted days, dwindled to hours, and finally ended after a mere 45 minutes of bidding. Jet planes, fax machines, and the internet revolutionized the tea business, allowing tea dealers to go right to the source or to auctions held near the world's major growing regions in Africa, India, China, and Sri Lanka. But I'm getting ahead of the story.

Shortly after the first public sale in London, tea experienced another step toward acceptance. A product is not truly Westernized until it is advertised, and such was the fate of tea when the first advertisement appeared on September 30, 1658, in London's *Mercurius Politicus:*

> That excellent, and by all Physitians approved, China drink, called by the Chineans, Tcha, by other nations Tay alias Tee, is sold at the Sultaness-Head, a Cophee-house in Sweetings Rents, by the Royal Exchange, London.

While tea was found in popular seventeenth-century English coffeehouses, women were not. English coffeehouses were exclusively for men and became gathering places for a melting pot of ideas, but opening the doors to women was not one of them. One's choice of coffeehouse often reflected a man's character as

English navigator Henry Hudson discovered North America's Hudson River and Hudson Bay while sailing for the Dutch East India Company in 1609. When Hudson and his crew returned to England, the government confiscated his ship and ordered Hudson to remain loyal to England and never serve another country again.

What part of confidante has that poor teapot played ever since the kindly plant was introduced among us. Why myriads of women have cried over it, to be sure! What sickbeds it has smoked by! What fevered lips have received refreshment from it! Nature meant very kindly by women when she made the tea plant; and with a little thought, what a series of pictures and groups the fancy may conjure up and assemble round the teapot and cup.

—William Makepeace Thackeray (1811–1863), Author

well as his politics. At the height of the coffeehouse's popularity in London, King Charles II tried unsuccessfully to ban them, condemning them as outlets for treasonous activities. Meanwhile, tea was finding its place in popular society with the help of King Charles' wife, Portuguese princess Catherine of Braganza, whom he married in 1662. Interestingly, the Portuguese were the first Europeans to reach the Orient by sea, and established a trading port with China years before the British or Dutch.

While coffeehouses were restricted to men, the tea gardens of the eighteenth century brought English ladies and gentlemen together for tea in a grand manner. Because the gardens were public, they provided two significant firsts for British society as: 1) a social gathering where anyone could attend, exclusive of class, and 2) a public event where women could socialize without reproach. The gardens were elaborate, and most importantly, quite fashionable. Guests dined and danced, amused with any variety of activities from concerts to gambling, even fireworks, contributing to tea's increasing credibility and explosive popularity. London had a number of popular tea gardens, including Vauxhall and Ranelagh Gardens.

While King Charles II and his wife Catherine of Braganza helped to inspire England's acceptance of tea, it was Anna, the Duchess of Bedford (1783–1857), who is credited with infusing the institution of afternoon tea. To quiet her hunger pains between lunch and a traditionally late dinner, the Duchess asked to be served a light meal with tea in the afternoon. The idea caught on quickly. Soon, afternoon tea evolved into a social affair where finely dressed ladies would gather to chitchat while sipping tea and dining on delicate crustless finger sandwiches, scones, and pastries. This was also called "low" tea, because the women would sit on sofas and chairs gathered around low tables set with fine china and linens.

"High" tea, also known as "meat tea," was a working-class tradition of a much more substantial and informal meal served with tea. Often, it was the main meal of the day consisting of hearty sandwiches, meat pies, and sweets. The "high" refers to how it was taken, perched on stool tops or standing at a counter. High and low tea also referred to the time of the afternoon when such events were held. Low tea was held earlier, or "lower" in the afternoon, between 3 and 5 P.M., while high tea occurred "higher" in the afternoon, between 6 and 7 P.M.

High or low, another member of nobility, John Montagu, the 4th Earl of Sandwich, helped make tea much more enjoyable. A British politician, Montagu served at different times between 1748 and 1782 as first lord of the admiralty and secretary of the state. He was also a patron of Captain James Cook, who discovered and named the Sandwich (Hawaiian) Islands after him. One of Montagu's greatest passions was gambling—apparently so much so that he did not want to leave the gaming table. Rather than stop for a formal meal, he ate meat between two slices of bread, creating the culinary tradition that bears his name and is the main course of afternoon tea. Today, John Montagu, the 11th Earl of Sandwich, carries on the family name and tradition in England by operating a sandwich catering business.

With tea's ease of preparation (coffee beans had to be roasted and ground), the reduction in tea taxes, and the aid of the clipper ships, which we will look at in the next chapter, tea became a more convenient, affordable, and available beverage—eventually replacing coffee and ale as England's drink of choice.

Tea Lands in America

Tea followed a similar history in America, where it appeared in the Dutch colony of New Amsterdam around the middle of the seventeenth century. When England took possession in 1674 and renamed the city New York, the American colonies were actually drinking more tea than all of England. At the height of its popularity, New York had impressive tea gardens fashioned after London's Vauxhall and Ranelagh Gardens, and much fuss was made over tea—even to the extent of developing special tea water pumps to provide suitable brewing water, which vendors sold on the streets.

The celebration of tea lasted nearly a century, until 1773, when American colonists, angry over taxes on British tea, hosted the world's most famous tea party in Boston Harbor (see Chapter 2). Tea consumption plummeted and soon

It was Queen Catherine's desire for the beloved brew that made tea a stylish drink among the English nobility, but the king also had some input. During the previous decade, King Charles II had spent eight years in exile at The Hague, the Netherlands, where he was exposed to the charms of tea. Together, the royal pair validated tea's use with the English citizenry.

the country was embroiled in war. It wasn't until after the American Revolution that tea consumption seriously resumed, and men like John Jacob Astor were happy to supply it. Astor was America's first millionaire, making part of his vast fortune in the tea trade.

At the end of the American Revolution, ten long years after the Boston Tea Party, Astor arrived in America. The son of a German farmer, his pockets were empty and he was hungry for success. He had heard there was money to be made in the fur trade, so at age 21, Astor began developing trading posts along the Missouri and Columbia rivers, buying furs directly from the Native Americans. He would send his furs to Europe and the Far East and the ships would return stocked with tea, feeding America's growing demand for tea and significantly increasing Astor's wealth. When he died in 1848, Astor was worth $20 million—or about $78 billion in today's value—making him the fourth wealthiest man in American history.

Astor's death came shortly after the start of the Victorian era, named for the sixty-three-year rule of England's Queen Victoria (1837–1901). This time of the longest royal reign in England's history was a time characterized by a very conservative morality that influenced literature, architecture, design, and even fashion. It was also a time when afternoon tea really took hold in America. In the late 1800s, "proper" ladies gathered in their parlors for small talk and tea in the style of England's "low" tea, and many hotels began elegant afternoon tea service. The popularity of these teas continued long after Queen Victoria's death in 1901.

Opened in 1907, New York's Plaza Hotel, and Boston's Ritz Carlton, which opened in 1927, gained reputations for stylish teas that continue to this day. Not long after the Plaza Hotel opened its doors, late afternoon tea dances popularizing current dance crazes became all the rage in America, a trend that was fashionable until World War II, and has regained some popularity in recent years. Much like the tea gardens of earlier years, tea dances provided a way for young, single women to mix with and meet men—without damaging their reputation. James Norwood Pratt, in the first edition of his timeless book, *Tea Lover's Treasury*, commented:

A 1764 advertisement for Ranelagh Gardens describes an evening where the orchestra will be "elegantly illuminated" and the fireworks with "several new transparent paintings and illuminations" will be "much superior to any thing of the kind ever given there before."

Yet nowhere in my study did I discover tea customs more bizarre than those prescribed for previous generations by Emily (Mrs. Price) Post. One of Mrs. Post's favorite subjects is the tea dance, for instance—from her description a likely opportunity to meet young men with no pressing need to make a living.

America ushered in the twentieth century with two important inventions that changed the way we drink tea: the tea bag and iced tea. In 1904, a quick-thinking Englishman created a new American tradition. It happened at the World's Fair in St. Louis, Missouri, when a tea merchant named Richard Blechynden reportedly couldn't even give away hot cups of tea to the sweltering fairgoers. In a moment of inspiration, it is said he decided to cool the tea by dropping ice into the cups. This created a sellout sensation and started a continuing appreciation that is uniquely American.

The American tea bag. It happened in St. Louis in 1904.

It is interesting to note that Japanese scholar and Oriental art expert, Kakuzo

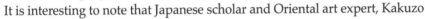

Standardizing Tea

Near the turn of the twentieth century, few standards existed for importing tea, allowing dishonest tea merchants to sell "tea" containing very little tea leaves. This prompted the federal government to step in and pass the Tea Act in 1897. The Act set minimum standards for importing tea and instituted a Board of Tea Experts known as the "tea tasters." The board met two days a year in Brooklyn to sip and sniff out only tea good enough to drink. In 1996, the seven-member board was a victim of budget cuts, putting an end to nearly a century of national tea tasters and saving the U.S. taxpayer $200,000 a year.

In 1899, following the passage of the Tea Act, the Tea Association of the USA was formed to represent the interests of the tea industry. In 1950, the Tea Council of the USA was created to promote and increase tea consumption. Later, reorganization combined the two under the direction of the Tea Association. Today, the Tea Association of the USA estimates it represents 80 percent of all tea traded in the United States.

The cozy fire is bright and gay, The merry kettle boils away and hums a cheerful song.

I sing the saucer and the cup; Pray, Mary, fill the teapot up, and do not make it strong.

—Barry Pain, Pen Name of English Author Eric Odell (1865–1928)

Okakura, was also at the 1904 World's Fair, where he was invited to speak at the International Conference of Culture and Literature. Okakura's acclaimed book, *The Book of Tea* (1906), explains the role of tea in Japanese society and introduced the West to Japanese culture, using tea as a symbol. One wonders if Blechynden had the opportunity to offer Okakura a cup of iced tea. If so, being the representative voice for the world's oldest and most revered tea ritual, did Okakura accept this brand-new American twist on the traditional infusion?

Not long after the World's Fair, New York coffee and tea merchant Thomas Sullivan used hand-sewn silk bags, rather than tins, as a simple and economical way to send tea samples to his customers. The response was overwhelmingly positive, but surprising, because his customers were more impressed with the bags than their contents. The orders poured in and the idea caught on. The easy-to-use pouches revolutionized the tea industry and turned the centuries-old ritual of preparing tea into an act of convenience. In a culture that thrives on quick fixes, it's not surprising that an American devised a way to achieve immediate tea gratification.

According to Tomislav Podreka, author of *The Evolution of American Tea Cul-*

Vanderbilt Teahouse

A twelfth-century Chinese temple in the United States? It would seem impossible, unless of course you're the former Mrs. William K. Vanderbilt, owner of two "cottages" in Newport, Rhode Island. To take advantage of her oceanfront location, Mrs. Vanderbilt decided to have a teahouse built in the rear of her multi-million dollar home, appropriately named Marble House (built with 500,000 cubic feet of marble). A simple structure resembling a Japanese teahouse would not do. Mrs. Vanderbilt sent her architects to China for an entire year to study temple architecture. Built in 1914, the Marble House Teahouse is said to be an excellent representation of twelfth-century Chinese temples. Ironically it was not used as a traditional teahouse. Mrs. Vanderbilt hosted some afternoon teas, but many evening parties and women's suffrage meetings.

ture and owner of Serendipitea, a company specializing in fine teas: "We are, as an industry, at the beginning of the establishment of an American tea ritual" (as printed in *Fresh Cup Magazine's Tea Almanac 2001*).

Great news for tea lovers: we are also at the beginning of an American tea boom. In the past several years, America's trend toward tea has inspired tea lovers and entrepreneurs to open tea shops and tearooms across the country, in every major city and many small ones. Tea enthusiasts can find everything from mom-and-pop storefronts tucked into strip malls, to oversized chic shops with less charm but trendier addresses. A popular website, the Cat-Tea Corner©, has over 2,000 listings and more than 800 reviews for tea shops and tearooms in every state, throughout Canada, and in more than forty different countries, proving that you are very likely never far from a good cup of tea.

But perhaps one of the best places to enjoy a comforting cuppa is right at home. The following wise words from poet William Cowper (1731–1800) conjure up a cozy scene that is just as easy to appreciate today as when it was written over two hundred years ago:

> Now stir the fire, and close the shutters fast,
> Let fall the curtains, wheel the sofa round,
> And while the bubbling and loud-hissing urn
> Throws up a steamy column and the cups
> That cheer but not inebriate, wait on each,
> So let us welcome peaceful evening in

In the next chapter we will look at how the demand for tea transformed international trade, turning the elusive leaf into the elixir of the ages for which wars were fought, fortunes made, and empires built. It is yet another chapter in tea's incredible journey from hilltop to tabletop. A journey that will take us from the Far East, across Europe and to the New World, where the lure of the leaf casts its spell on revolutionaries and rebels, entrepreneurs and empire builders alike.

"They offered us tea and bread, and were quite joyous their part of the war was over."

—American soldier, near Baghdad
April 2, 2003

CHAPTER 2

From**Port**Dock to**Teapot**

*Tea represents both the prestigious and the common
and is found in the shanties of the ghettos as well as
the pantries of the wealthy. It holds no social standings
and it is seen the world over as an egalitarian beverage.*

—TOMISLAV PODREKA
THE EVOLUTION OF AMERICAN TEA CULTURE

O ver a trillion cups of tea are consumed worldwide every year. In the United States alone, tea is over a $5-billion-a-year industry, accounting for more than 125 million cups or glasses of tea per day. Approximately half the American population drinks tea every day, and you'll find some form of tea in almost 80 percent of American households.

In England, each day over 70 percent of the population above age 10 drinks tea, accounting for about 165 million cups, or nearly half of all drinks consumed daily. And according to a national poll, a surprising 92 percent of Canadian women and 87 percent of Canadian men are tea drinkers. But it is the Irish who

May you always be blessed with walls for the wind, A roof for the rain, A warm cup of tea by the fire, Laughter to cheer you, Those you love near you, And all that your heart might desire.

—Old Gaelic Blessing

drink the most tea per capita, annually consuming about six pounds of tea per person. While these numbers sound impressive, the West swallows up only a small percentage of the world's tea. Together India, China, and Japan drink nearly half the world's annual tea consumption. India is both the world's largest tea producer and its largest consumer.

In 2002, the world's top five tea-exporting countries of Sri Lanka, Kenya, China, India, and Indonesia shipped over 1 million metric tons of tea from their ports. The top tea importer, the Russian Federation, has honored tea (as well as vodka) as its national drink.

So how did tea, once a little known treasure from the Far East, find its way to every continent? How did this once exotic elixir become almost as popular as water? The universal acceptance of tea followed the sweeping success of the tea trade. Read on to learn how the love for the leaf crossed all cultural barriers and fueled a ruthless race of international proportions to conquer the world's craving for tea.

ENGLAND'S *UN*-HONORABLE EAST INDIA COMPANY

England's Queen Elizabeth I chartered the Honorable East India Company, also known as the John Company, on December 31, 1600. Its goal was to promote Asian trade. However, it became the foundation for the British Empire, the most powerful monopoly the world has ever seen, at its peak controlling 20 percent of the world's land area and more than 400 million people. And the source for all this power and influence? Merely tea. But it didn't begin that way. At its inception, the English East India Company set out to destroy the Dutch's grip on the East Indies spice trade, but later found there was much more money to be made in tea leaves than cinnamon, cloves, pepper, and nutmeg.

So, for nearly two hundred years, the importation of tea fueled the East India Company's unchecked quest for domination of the tea trade and the world. The company's success was significantly aided by the far-reaching powers bestowed on it, including the ability to take and control territory; manufacture money; declare war; and pass laws, judgment, and punishment. The company

The entire British Empire was built on cups of tea. . . . And if you think I'm going to war without one you're sadly mistaken.

—*Lock, Stock and Two Smoking Barrels* Written and directed by Guy Ritchie, 1998

could flex England's muscle through a path of power that included all trade east of the Cape of Good Hope and west of Cape Horn—basically everywhere from present-day South Africa to South America.

Fiercely competitive with the Dutch, French, and the Portuguese, the English East India Company reached the Chinese port of Macau, seventy miles south of Canton in 1637. The Portuguese were the first Europeans to establish trade at Macau eighty years earlier, and in fact, Macau remained the last European colony in Asia until it was returned to Chinese control in 1999. In 1684, the English East India Company was allowed to build a factory near Canton, which shortly thereafter became the singular port from which the Manchu emperor allowed trade with the "foreign devils." He devised the Canton system, providing a way for the Chinese to profit from the lucrative European trade with the least amount of contact with the "white barbarians." The emperor appointed an official who selected merchants called the Cohong. The Cohong, who never numbered more than thirteen, conducted all the business with the traders.

England Craves the Leaf

With London's first public sale of tea at Thomas Garway's Coffeehouse in 1657, and the royal tea-drinking couple of King Charles II and his wife Catherine leading the country, tea use began a slow and steady increase in England. By 1689, London began directly importing tea from China, and by 1700 about 20,000 pounds were imported each year. In twenty-five years, that number increased over ten times to 250,000 pounds, and by 1800 England annually imported an average 24 million pounds of tea.

Actually, those are just the official numbers of England's East India Company. The real accounting of tea could be as much as one-half to two-thirds greater. The hold the Company had on the English tea trade allowed them to heavily tax its importation—as much as five shillings per two shillings worth of tea. The inflated prices resulted in decades of black market tea, secreted into the country by smugglers whose illegal contraband was welcomed by much of the

The progress of this famous plant has been something like the progress of truth; suspected at first, though very palatable to those who had courage to taste it; resisted as it encroached; abused as its popularity seemed to spread; and establishing its triumph at last, in cheering the whole land from the palace to the cottage, only by the slow and restless efforts of time and its own virtues.

—Isaac D'Israeli (1766–1848), English Author

people. It also led to the nasty practice of adulteration. Much like a dishonest bartender who waters down a customer's drink, shady tea traders would mix tea leaves with sawdust, tree leaves, even gunpowder to increase the supply and meet the demand for more and more tea.

World's Most Famous Tea Party

Meanwhile, the tempest in the teapot was beginning to brew across the Atlantic Ocean in the New World, where the turmoil over taxation was reaching the boiling point. The English East India Company had allowed itself to be ravaged from the inside out by years of mismanagement, inefficiency, and embezzle-

ment. With its warehouses teeming with tea leaves and the Company teetering on the brink of ruin, the Honorable East India Company looked to British Parliament for salvation. Parliament responded by passing the Tea Act of 1773, which gave the Company the authority to ship tea duty free from England to America, where the tax would be added before it was sold. Even with the tax, it would still be cheaper than smuggled Dutch tea. But at a time when the bottom line meant more than just the best deal, the colonists expressed their displeasure at taxation

The Boston Tea Party

without representation by throwing a tea party—literally.

On December 16, 1773, Samuel Adams led a group of about fifty men called the Sons of Liberty, many of whom were disguised as Native Americans. The men boarded three British ships anchored in Boston Harbor at Griffin's Wharf, and proceeded to throw 342 chests of tea into the harbor. Seemingly overnight, the Boston Tea Party and similar acts at other ports turned tea drinkers into traitors, and coffee became America's drink of choice—but that's another story.

The Cost of Tea

Back in England, the East India Company was still hanging on, but it was about to be dealt a blow led by Richard Twining, grandson of Thomas Twining, founder

Tea Travels to Russia

The same year the East India Company began directly importing tea to London from China, the Russians began their own tea trade with the Chinese. However, instead of cargo chests stashed in the bottom of seafaring ships, the tea traveled in cloth sacks atop camel caravans. In 1689 the Trade Treaty of Newchinsk established a common border between Russia and China, opening the over-land route, in which Russian furs were traded for Chinese tea. It was a seemingly impossible 11,000-mile, sixteen-month journey through China and across Mongolia. The final 1,000-mile stretch took 200 to 300 camels, each carrying up to 600 pounds of tea, through the harsh Gobi Desert. Importing tea in this slow, limited manner made tea a very expensive commodity. But by the time the Trans-Siberian Railroad replaced the caravans in 1900, the journey was cut from months to weeks and Russians were importing more tea than England.

While technology improved the means of tea transportation, the method of tea preparation changed little in Russia. Since the seventeenth century, the traditional Russian teapot, called the samovar, has been the symbol of home and hospitality. Designed to provide hot tea throughout the day, the large metal urn holds and heats the water on the bottom, while the teapot on top brews and keeps it hot using a tea concentrate. A metal pipe runs vertically through the middle to heat both containers, and tea is served by diluting the concentrate on top with boiled water from the main container. An old Russian saying, "to have a sit by a samovar," means to enjoy an unhurried talk while drinking tea from a samovar.

Samovars come in a variety of shapes and sizes, from quarts to gallons, cylindrical to spherical and plain to polished. Some samovars are intricate works of art; others are simply designed to work hard. Originally handmade, the first samovars to be commercially manufactured were made in the city of Tula, south of Moscow, which quickly established itself as the capital of samovar production. Even though other major cities attempted to compete, Tula retained its lead in the industry—so much so, that the Russian writer Anton Chekhov coined the phrase "to take one's own samovar to Tula," which is another way of saying "you're wasting your time." This phrase is still in use today. Samovar is derived from the Russian words *samo* (self) and *varit'* (to boil).

of the famous tea company bearing his name. As Chairman of the London Tea Dealers, Richard led a successful campaign against the crippling tea taxes, and convinced young Prime Minister William Pitt, only 25 years old and barely in power a year, to lower tea taxes. This effectively eliminated tea smugglers and more than doubled legitimate tea imports.

Of course, as the demand for tea increased, so did the cost. The Chinese wanted to be paid in silver and very little else the British had to offer. So the British decided to level the balance of trade by bargaining in lives for the leaves, and the price was costly indeed.

The East India Company was building an empire in India, and India had one thing the company could use to buy all the tea in China: opium. The company had factories in Calcutta and Madras (Chennai) and controlled the port city of Bombay (Mumbai), a property acquired as part of the wedding dowry when King Charles II married the King of Portugal's sister, Catherine of Braganza. Opium could be grown cheaply in its native India, and the East India Company used middlemen to do their dirty work—traders who would buy the opium in Calcutta and sell it in Canton for silver. The middlemen would then use the silver to pay their accounts with the company, who would, in turn, use the same silver to purchase tea from the Chinese.

In 1834, due to pressure from independent tea traders back home, the East India Company lost its monopoly in the China trade, but the coming Opium Wars would secure its strength in the area for many years. China could see that opium was creating a growing plague of addiction in the country, and wanted its importation stopped. The whole matter escalated into conflicts known as the Opium Wars. In 1842 and 1856, after defeat by the British, China signed treaties that ended the Canton system of Cohong merchants, secured additional trading ports and rights for British citizens, legalized opium, and opened more cities to foreign traders, travelers, and missionaries. The legalized importation of opium remained in effect until 1908. It is clear that opium and tea influenced each other during this time in China's history.

INDIA'S TEA INDUSTRY

Even though the tea plant, *Camellia sinensis,* is native to India as well as China, it wasn't until the East India Company lost its monopoly in the China tea trade that it began to look elsewhere for a place to cultivate its cash crop. The irony is that it found it in India—growing wild in the very soil that the company had been stepping all over for 170 years. While the company finally recognized India's tea-growing potential, it discredited the quality of the native tea plants first discovered growing wild in the forests of northeast India's Assam region. Instead, the company pursued the much more difficult, and ultimately disastrous, course of seeking seeds from China.

Scotsman Robert Fortune was a natural for this job. His previous success in China and his reputation as a plant hunter and adventurer made him the East India Company's choice to go deep into China's interior and bring back seeds, plants, and Chinese workmen for the new India tea gardens. He succeeded in 1851, but unfortunately the results of Fortune's arduous effort were fruitless. The cultivation of the Chinese tea plants was a bungled disaster.

It was the levelheaded wisdom of two men, Charles Bruce and George Williamson, who saved India's tea industry. Bruce is credited with establishing the tea industry in Assam. He discovered the wild tea plants with his brother deep in India's Assam forests as early as the 1820s, and always believed the company should cultivate native Assam plants, not the Chinese plants. Bruce went so far as to develop his own experimental tea garden, some of which was successfully auctioned in London in 1839, the same year London investors established the Assam Company and named Bruce superintendent.

But against his best judgment, Bruce was directed to cultivate the Chinese plants. It was an uphill battle and luck was not on Bruce's side. After years of struggles, sickness, and failure, Bruce was blamed for the bungled mess, ending his career with the Assam Company. It wasn't until Williamson took over in 1853 that he followed Bruce's lead, discovering that the quality and quantity of the Assam tea plants grown in their native soil was far superior to the transplanted

So hear it then, Rennie dear, Nor hear it with a frown;

You cannot make tea so fast as I can gulp it down.

I therefore pray thee, Rennie dear, that thou wilt give to me,

With cream and sugar softened well, another dish of tea.

—Samuel Johnson (1709–1784), Author/Lexicographer

Ta-Ta, Tetley!

In 1858, after the revolt of India's sepoy troops (also known as the Sepoy Rebellion and the Indian Mutiny), British Parliament dissolved the English East India Company and took over direct rule of the empire until Indian independence in 1947. But you might say that Tata Tea—one of the best-known tea brands in India and a subsidiary of the Tata Group, one of India's largest publicly quoted companies with diverse interests, including tea— had the last word on centuries of English domination when they purchased The Tetley Group for $433.6 million in 2000. Tetley was one of the early English tea companies, founded in 1837, years before the success of India's tea industry. Now, Tata Tea is one of the largest tea companies in the world.

Chinese tea. Williamson also recognized growing conditions were different from China and he instituted changes in harvesting methods for the India tea bushes, allowing them to grow longer before plucking, which provided greater yields. Now, India is the world's largest tea producer, and Assam is one of the world's best and most popular teas. But there is even more to Williamson's story.

George's little brother, Captain James Hay Williamson, was a former steamship captain turned tea grower and tea agent. In 1866, the Captain met R.B. Magor at the Great Eastern Hotel in Calcutta, where Magor was an assistant. They formed a partnership in 1869 as business agents for tea estates and investors in tea cultivation and production. In the 1870s, George joined his brother and R.B. Magor as a third partner. Williamson Magor & Co. worked closely with its London partner George Williamson & Co., and together grew to hold a considerable share in the Indian tea industry—producing about 47 million kilograms of tea a year. In April 2001 the partnership ended and the companies became the George Williamson (Assam) Ltd. and the Williamson Magor Group. George Williamson Ltd. has seventeen tea estates in India, producing about 20 million kilograms annually. The Williamson Magor Group has twenty-eight tea estates there, producing about 35 million kilograms of tea annually.

THE RACE FOR TEA

Blind to its impending demise, the English East India Company was struggling to get the fledgling India tea business to turn a profit in 1849 when Parliament dealt it another blow by repealing the Navigation Acts. The acts had allowed only British vessels to ship goods to the colonies. Now, America could compete directly with the British, who were centuries ahead in the lucrative China tea trade. America had to race to catch up, and that is exactly what she did.

In order to compete, the Americans needed an edge, something the British didn't have. The answer came in the new clipper ships, the fastest sailing vessels ever built. Averaging 185 feet in length, the magnificent three-masted ships with iron-strapped frames were strong, but lean. Designed to carry cargoes of high value but small volume, they sacrificed cargo space for speed. And it was the speed that mattered, because top prices were paid for the first Chinese tea to reach London, and bonuses were given to the accomplished crew. The clippers easily out-sailed England's "tea wagons," so with fortunes at stake, the British built their own clipper ships and the race was on.

The *Cutty Sark*

The most famous British clipper ship, the *Cutty Sark*, was launched in 1869. Unfortunately, that was the same year the Suez Canal opened, cutting a quicker route for steamships to reach the Far East and eventually ending the clipper's role in the tea trade. Ownership of the *Cutty Sark*, as well as her name, changed hands a couple of times, but she was eventually rescued by an old sailor, Captain Wilfred Dowman, who bought the battered ship in 1922 and restored her to her original glory. His widow donated the ship to the Thames Nautical Training College and in 1952 the Cutty Sark Preservation Society was founded. Two years later, the ship had a permanent home at a custom-built dry dock in Greenwich, England, where she remains today. Over 15 million people have visited the *Cutty Sark*, the world's only surviving tea clipper.

The era of the clipper ships and tea races in the 1850s and 1860s was an exciting period in tea's sometimes shameful history. The inspiring image of a graceful tall ship streaming up London's Thames River to cheering crowds briefly overshadows the previous years punctuated by plundering, smuggling, thievery, opium-trading, and greed. While the development of the steamship ended the clipper's reign in the 1870s, nothing will replace its stature on the high seas.

THE BUSINESS OF TEA

All the time and toil it took to deliver tea from halfway around the world to London's docks is only part of the story. Reaching the hearths of the people is the other. The tea aisle of your favorite store hints at the long history of marketing tea from the port dock to the teapot. A few of the most recognizable names—Twining, Tetley, and Lipton—still stand on store shelves. Despite the elimination of the monopolizing English East India Company, tea remains a money-making big business commodity. Corporate acquisitions of tea brands are very much a part of the modern tale of tea.

Early British Tea Merchants

Early English masters of the tea trade made a lasting name for themselves. Throughout the past three centuries and way beyond, Great Britain's tea traders have infused the business of tea with an entrepreneurial spirit that has created a lingering strength and set the standard for success.

Twining

Thomas Twining came from a long line of wool weavers and trained to continue the trade until 1701, when at the age of 26, he broke family tradition to try something completely different—handling imports, including tea, for an English East India Company merchant. Twining's interest in tea led him to purchase London's Tom's Coffee House just five years later. Like many coffeehouses of the time, his sold tea as a specialty item. However, as tea's popularity grew, so did Tom Twining's. In 1717, after buying the three bordering buildings, he started England's first dry tea and coffee shop at 216 Strand. Actually, the address was assigned much later, but the location is home to the original and still-operating tea shop and Twinings museum. By 1734, Thomas dropped the coffee business and focused totally on tea. His customers included society's lords and ladies, and even Queen Anne and King George I.

His son, Daniel, expanded the business by exporting tea to America as early as 1749. When Daniel died, his wife Mary Little ran the company for nearly twenty years, until she turned it over to her son, Thomas. As we've already learned, Thomas helped chip away at the English East India Company's power when he played a key role in ending the paralyzing tea taxes in 1784. In 1964, Twinings was purchased by Associated British Foods, but it remains family run. Ten generations and nearly 300 years later, R. Twining and Company, Ltd. continues to weave its tale of tea in 100 countries around the world.

Tetley

Another prominent early English tea company with humble beginnings is Tetley. The Tetley brothers, Joseph and Edward, were orphaned teenagers who started out hawking salt and later tea to villages in Northern England until they raised enough money to become proper tea merchants in 1837. They opened shop in London in 1856, but the brothers were unable to agree, so Edward left. Joseph acquired a partner and Joseph Tetley & Company, Wholesale Tea Dealers was created. In 1888 Tetley expanded operations into America. The company's success attracted J. Lyons & Co., proprietors of England's first teahouse—which grew into a wildly successful chain and tea company, of which tea was just one of many products that even included Baskin-Robbins Ice Cream.

J. Lyons & Co. acquired Tetley in 1973, forming Lyons Tetley, Ltd. However, J. Lyons' shaky financial future forced the sale to Allied Breweries in 1978. Over the years, Allied-Lyons sold and merged pieces of the J. Lyons Company and

Even Yale University has a history steeped in tea. Its namesake and benefactor, Elihu Yale, made his fortune working for the tea-trading empire of the British East India Company. When the Collegiate School of Connecticut was about to move to New Haven, Yale was persuaded by his step-grandfather to make a generous donation that allowed for the construction of the Yale College building. In 1999 the university celebrated Yale's 350th birthday with cake, and of course, iced tea.

acquired other companies, especially in the beverage trade. The 1994 purchase of Pedro Domecq, a leading spirits company in Spain and Mexico, turned the focus of the company, now called Allied Domecq, to the spirits and retailing business. This focus prompted Allied Domecq to sell their tea interests, which eventually led to India's Tata Tea's purchase of The Tetley Group in 2000, making it one of the largest international tea companies, second only to Unilever.

Lipton

Lipton tea is one of the most popular and well-recognized teas in America. Sir Thomas Lipton was an entrepreneur extraordinaire, a millionaire by the age of 29. In 1865 at the age of 15, Lipton left his home in Glasgow, Scotland, and sailed to America, where he learned the grocery trade in New York City. He returned to Glasgow four years later with a little savings and a lot of determination. At the age of 21, Lipton opened his first grocery store, where he parlayed his genius for advertising and willingness to work hard into a successful chain of grocery stores. By the age of 40, he owned 300 grocery stores in Great Britain. Naturally, he began looking for new ventures.

A shrewd businessman with an eye for opportunity, Lipton took advantage of a blight that destroyed the coffee plantations of Ceylon (Sri Lanka). He bought the land at a bargain price and turned the plantations into tea-growing estates. Then, he undercut the competition, selling the tea to his customers at a considerable discount and touting it as "the finest the world can produce." In the process, Lipton helped turn Sri Lanka into one of the world's top tea-producing countries. In 2002, Sri Lanka was the third-largest producer of tea, but the single largest exporter, exporting 285,985 metric tons compared to Kenya's export of 267,721 metric tons and China's 252,273 metric tons.

A typical tea field.

Now, Lipton is one of many companies owned by Unilever, an international giant with operations in eighty countries selling products in over 150 nations and employing about 265,000 people. Unilever also owns Canada's favorite tea company, Red Rose, which it acquired with the purchase of Brooke Bond in 1984. At

Lipton the Sailor

Ever wonder why packages of Lipton tea always show Sir Thomas Lipton pictured with a sailor's hat on? Tea multiplied Lipton's millions and extended his fame well beyond Great Britain. In 1909, he opened a factory in New York, the beginning of his tremendous success in the United States. However, Lipton did not succeed at his ultimate challenge—winning the America's Cup yacht race. The old sailor tried five times; his last attempt was in 1930 at the age of 80.

the time, Brooke Bond was the world's largest tea company. Unilever also owns England's popular PG Tips tea, Ireland's Lyons tea, and India's Red Label tea.

American Tea Companies

Successful American tea entrepreneurs emerged in the twentieth century that changed the way we think about tea. Indeed, these are some of the most innovative tea companies in business today.

R.C. Bigelow, Inc.

In the 1940s, Ruth Bigelow was a woman ahead of her time. A generation before women demanded equal rights, at a time when many thought a woman's place was in the home, Ruth Bigelow was busy building one of America's most successful tea companies. Pursuing her idea of the perfect cup of tea, Ruth was searching for a better blend when she found an old colonial recipe with orange peels and spices. Working in her New York kitchen, she created a tea that generated "constant comments," thus the name for her signature tea, Constant Comment. By 1945, Ruth was packaging and shipping her tea and by 1950, she opened Bigelow's first factory in Connecticut. In 1958, she bought Bigelow's first tea bag machine. Sixty years later, R.C. Bigelow, Inc. is run by Ruth's son, David, and is one of the few remaining family-run tea companies. Offering a wide variety of teas, Bigelow has manufacturing and distributing facilities in Connecticut, Idaho, and Kentucky, and claims to sell over a billion cups of tea per year.

Celestial Seasonings

While Ruth Bigelow started her company testing recipes in her kitchen, one of her major competitors, Celestial Seasonings, began with fieldwork—literally. A child of the 1960s, teenager Mo Siegel and his friends were picking wild herbs in the Rocky Mountains in 1968. By 1969, the same year Woodstock packed thousands into a farm field in upstate New York, Mo and his friends had hand-picked enough herbs to pack 10,000 muslin bags with Mo's 36 Herb Tea, which they sold to a Boulder, Colorado health food store. By 1970, they had six employees working out of a Boulder barn. Mo realized if the company was going to grow he was going to have to get out of the field and let someone else do the picking, so he started buying herbs from around the world. Within five years of starting the company, Celestial had sales of over $1 million and was providing its nearly fifty employees with free vegetarian lunches and instituted lunch-time volleyball games. Twenty-five years later, Celestial had 270 employees and sales of over $100 million.

Teacups to Court Dockets

Celestial Seasonings was sold to Kraft Foods, Inc. in 1984. But four years later, when Kraft tried to sell Celestial Seasonings to Thomas J. Lipton, Inc., Bigelow stepped in and cried foul, challenging the sale with anti-trust litigation. At the time, Celestial Seasonings owned about half the herbal tea market and Lipton had about another 18 percent, to Bigelow's approximately 17 percent. The merger would have created a company with nearly 70 percent of North America's herbal tea market. Celestial Seasonings decided to buy the company back from Kraft in 1988.

Trippin' Tea

President Richard Nixon didn't have a clue how close he came to what could have been his most unforgettable trip, and he wouldn't have even left the White House. All he had to do was sip a cup of tea.

A popular story is told that Grace Slick, vocalist with the rock group Jefferson Airplane, was invited to a tea party at the White House on April 24, 1970. It was given by President Nixon's daughter Tricia for alumni of Finch College. Ms. Slick thought it would be a fine idea to secretly slip LSD into the President's teacup. Colorless and odorless, it would have been undetectable. So Ms. Slick headed to the world's most famous house with the LSD tucked in her pocket. She also brought along Abbie Hoffman, well-known social and political activist and leader of the Youth International Party (Yippies), as her bodyguard and escort. Unfortunately for Ms. Slick, her plan was foiled by White House security who denied Mr. Hoffman entrance to the female-only party. Slick left with him, but what a party it might have been!

Celestial Seasonings sued Bigelow in 1995, citing Bigelow with practicing false advertising and package-design infringement. Celestial claimed they lost $70 million in sales and damages and that Bigelow did not indicate some of their teas contained artificial flavorings. Although a judge ultimately ruled against Celestial Seasonings' claims, Mo Siegel expressed a little victory when he noted that Bigelow had since changed some of their package labeling.

In 2000, Celestial Seasonings was sold to the Hain Food Group, a major natural food brand company, creating The Hain Celestial Group. Celestial Seasonings' herbal, traditional, bottled, and medicinal teas and herbal supplements are sold in over forty countries and the group claims to serve more than 1.2 billion cups of tea per year.

A Healthy Niche

Good Earth Teas has been around nearly as long as Celestial Seasonings. Founded

Southern Comfort

June is National Iced Tea Month in the United States. As spring slips into summer and the warm days stretch into the evening hours, it is a perfect time to champion the charms of this classic American drink. As a beverage, tea is nearly 5,000 years old, but iced tea, a distinctly American drink, is in its infancy. Just over 100 years old, it was created in the middle of summer, in the middle of America, at the 1904 World's Fair in St. Louis, Missouri, by an English merchant who dropped ice into hot cups of tea to tempt sweltering fair-goers. It was an idea that was an instant success, especially in the South, where it is estimated half of all the iced tea in the United States is consumed—over 16 billion glasses a year. Greeting guests with a refreshing glass of iced tea is a welcome tradition in the South. Even long after the invention of air conditioning, iced tea remains a Southern comfort and natural icebreaker. In fact, some politicians would like to make it a law. Not to drink iced tea, but to sweeten it.

In the spring of 2003, several Georgia State representatives introduced a bill that would make it a law that any Georgia restaurant serving iced tea must also serve sweet iced tea. It even stipulated the tea must be sweetened when brewed. One of the sponsors of the bill, Representative John Noel, said it was all in fun. But if the bill became law, it would be a misdemeanor not to offer sweet tea, punishable by up to twelve months in jail. Not exactly a sweet deal for an offending establishment!

in 1972 by husband and wife Ben Zaricor and Louise Veninga, Good Earth Teas is a division of the Fmali Herb Company. A popular American brand offering a variety of teas, the company has developed a niche market of imported medicinal teas (reportedly made from traditional Swiss formulas) manufactured in Europe for over seventy-five years. Good Earth Teas has also branched out into the restaurant business with an emphasis on healthy food.

Yogi Tea actually evolved from a string of health food restaurants—and a tea recipe from a real yogi. The man behind the brand is Yogi Bhajan. The tea served by his students in Golden Temple Vegetarian Restaurants was reportedly so popular it stirred up enough interest to start the Yogi Tea Company in 1984. The company has expanded to offer over forty different varieties of tea including several "healing formulas" using organic green tea.

One of the newest tea companies with a healthy and environment-friendly focus is Honest Tea. Its all-natural, ready-to-drink bottled teas have been on store shelves since the summer of 1998, the result of the collaboration of Seth Goldman and his former Yale University professor, Barry Nalebuff. The two were seeking to fill the void in the alternative beverage market between drinks that were too sweet and those with no flavor. Honest Tea is made with only limited amounts of organic sugar or organic honey and no artificial sweeteners, flavors, or colors. In 2000, the company introduced whole-leaf tea made with a unique biodegradable tea bag and tag design. Several varieties of Honest Tea are fully organic and labeled USDA Organic (see the organic tea discussion in Chapter 4).

Fresh tea leaves.

Northwest Stirs Up the Tea Industry

Tea is probably not what comes to mind when you think of the Pacific Northwest. Home to Mount St. Helens and the Space Needle, the Pacific Northwest is considered by many as America's coffee capitol, mainly because it spawned Seattle's super-sized Starbucks chain. With an accelerated growth plan seemingly wired on too many Grande triple espressos and fueled with annual sales of over $4 bil-

A Booming Bottled Tea Industry

An estimated 80 percent of tea consumed in the United States is iced tea, and ready-to-drink (RTD) bottled tea is the fastest growing segment of the tea industry. According to Joseph Simrany, President of the Tea Association of the USA, in a report titled, "The State of the U.S. Tea Industry," the RTD tea category alone accounted for an estimated $1.8 billion in United States sales in 2001, up from $200 million in 1990. Mr. Simrany predicts the market for RTD tea will continue to grow by eight to ten percent over the next several years. With increased marketing, RTD tea may even brew up a larger jump.

lion, Starbucks opens three to four new stores every day around the world and expects to have 10,000 stores in sixty countries soon. Its long-term global goal is 25,000 stores. That news may be tough to swallow for John Winter Smith, a software developer from Dallas, Texas, who's made it his life's goal to visit every one. On a "good" day he might gulp down as many as twenty-five cups of coffee. Is it the challenge of completing a seemingly impossible task or just all that caffeine pumping through his veins that compels him to continue? Something to consider over a good cup of tea—and Starbucks does sell good tea. Just where it comes from may surprise you.

Often overshadowed by its Seattle neighbor, Portland, Oregon (just 170 miles south), is the specialty tea industry's corporate home to multi-million dollar success stories—Stash Tea, Tazo Tea, Oregon Chai, and Kombucha Wonder Drink.

The Top Tea Place of the Year Awards

You've heard of the Academy Awards for acting, but how about for the perfect cup of tea? Each summer, The Tea Council of the United Kingdom announces The Top Tea Place of the Year Award. Nicknamed the "Oscar" of The Tea Council's awards, it is a prestigious distinction achieved only after successfully meeting an extensive list of criteria. Once a teahouse has been nominated, secret tea-tasters are sent out to evaluate each establishment. In a country that enjoys its tea drinking enormously, the Tea Council takes its job seriously. Its judging criteria include the following:

1. Quality of tea used and range of teas on offer.
2. Method of making tea and temperature at which it is served.
3. Appearance of the liquor and taste.
4. Availability of fresh milk on offer or lemon, type of sugar, and how it is presented.
5. Condition of the crockery, general cleanliness, and hygiene of the outlet.
6. The efficiency, helpfulness, and attitude of the staff.
7. The quality of the food, overall value for money, and the overall ambience of the outlet.

Here, you will also find the Starbucks connection, because Tazo Tea sealed a deal with Starbucks in January 1999 to be the exclusive provider of teas in all their stores. The sale, a reported $9.1 million, had an immediate effect, sending Tazo scrambling for space, doubling its tea purchases and taking the tiny tea company of twenty-three employees into the fold of North America's largest coffee retailer with (at the time) 2,000 stores, 28,000 employees, and over $1 billion in annual sales. The deal put Tazo Tea within reach of an estimated one million premium coffee consumers every day, but allowed Tazo to retain its own identity and independence.

Reinventing Tea

Steve Smith, an innovator in the tea industry, is the president of Tazo and the man behind the deal. Smith was also on the ground floor of Portland's Stash Tea Company in the early 1970s, which got its start selling herbal tea to natural food stores out of an old Victorian house. By the mid-1970s, Stash was the first company to introduce a full line of herbals and specialty tea to the college and restaurant markets. One of the top specialty tea companies in the United States, Stash is at the forefront of tea businesses experimenting with tea as a cooking ingredient. Several recipes in this book were created in Stash's test kitchens.

After Stash was purchased by an overseas company in the early 1990s, Smith decided it was time for a change. He started Tazo in 1993 and tagged it "The Reincarnation of Tea." Combining quality tea and unique presentation, he built a brand identity with a mystical appeal. Tazo's cryptic lettering resembles etchings lifted from an ancient cave wall, giving the product a mystique that hints at secret knowledge, while offering up bits of wisdom on the packaging. When Starbucks purchased Tazo, Howard Schultz, Starbucks' chairman and chief global strategist, noted the increasing marketability of tea when he commented in Portland's newspaper, *The Oregonian*, "Tea will drive more people into our stores."

The Republic of Tea is another young American tea company changing the image of tea. Founded in 1992, it has created a unique identity based on an imag-

In an interesting twist, at the same time Starbucks announced the purchase of Tazo and its plans to bring tea to its coffee customers, Starbucks also announced the opening of its first coffee outlet in the very birthplace of tea—China. Within five years, Starbucks opened over 100 stores in China.

inary land where sales outlets are embassies, employees are ministers and ambassadors, and customers are Citizens of The Republic. It is the company's mission to create a Tea Revolution of "TeaMinded" Citizens "that will enrich the lives of our Citizens through the sip by sip rather than gulp by gulp life—a life of health, balance and well-being."

Maybe the future of tea is in companies like Steep. The brainchild of Jeff Piazza, Steep sells whole-leaf tea in innovative matchbox packages that are designed to appeal to the next generation of tea drinkers. Steep's "hip" focus on design and attitude appeals to young people through its website and by its presence in cool places like small, independent coffeehouses and cafes where it is a "hip sip" (hmm, sounds groovy). Piazza believes his customers will willingly pay more for whole-leaf tea versus a tea bag, which he says is like comparing steak to hamburger. In business since 1995, his growing success with customers like MTV and offers for big dollar corporate buyouts proves there must be a trend brewing.

What's next for the tea industry? In just over ten years, from 1990 to 2003, American sales have more than doubled from $1.8 billion to over $5.1 billion, and are estimated to reach $10 billion by 2010. Clearly, the internet will be part of tea's future; already every major tea company operates a website (see "Tea Companies" in the Resource List, beginning on page 169). With innovative marketing, increased awareness of tea's health benefits (see Chapter 5), and the growing availability of premium loose leaf, bagged, and bottled teas, the love of the leaf looks poised to continue for at least another 5,000 years.

CHAPTER 3

What's It All About?

*When the water is boiling, it must look like the fishes' eyes
and give off but the hint of sound. When at the edges it
chatters like a bubbling spring and looks like pearls
innumerable strung together, it has reached the second stage.
When it leaps like breakers majestic and resounds
like a swelling wave, it is at its peak. Anymore and
the water will be boiled out and should not be used.*

—LU YU, *THE CLASSIC OF TEA*

In the hundreds of years since Lu Yu wrote his poetic passage describing the ideal temperature for tea water, there has been no shortage of opinions on how best to brew the perfect cup of tea. But before discussing how to prepare tea, let's consider exactly what tea is.

The very name, "tea," is unique to the Western world. It is known as *cha* or *chai* in many countries, a matter of dialect and a result of the earliest trade routes that brought tea to Europe. As mentioned in Chapter 1, the Dutch introduced tea to Europe in 1610. Before China allowed them to establish trading ports in Macau

The tea plant, *Camellia sinensis*, just happens to be the next of kin to the Alabama state flower, the common garden-flowering Camellia (*Camellia japonica*). The Camellia replaced goldenrod as the state flower in 1959 after the Men's Camellia Club in Greenville took up the charge, arguing for the plant's commercial importance to the state for nursery growers and tourism.

and Canton, the Dutch operated from the island of Java in Indonesia, trading with merchants from Amoy (Xiamen) in southeastern China's Fujian province, located across from the island of Taiwan. In the Amoy dialect, tea is *T'e*, pronounced "tay," the name still used in many European countries. *Cha*, often called *chai*, is the Cantonese word for tea and how tea is referred to in places like Russia, India, and the Middle East.

Tea, tay, cha, or chai, whatever the name, there are nearly 3,000 varieties available today. All are derived from one plant, a warm-weather evergreen shrub native to China, Tibet, and northern India called *Camellia sinensis*, the internationally recognized botanical name for the plant. *Camellia* comes from G. J. Camellus, a Jesuit missionary who brought the plant to Europe from Asia in the seventeenth century. *Sinensis* is Latin, and indicates that the species was originally found in China.

TEA CATEGORIES

There are two types of tea bushes, or *jat*: China jat and Indian, or Assam jat. The term refers to the origin of the plant's seeds or cuttings. The Assam leaf is larger, more prolific, and more sensitive to the cold than the China leaf. Contrary to popular belief, there are no "black tea bushes" or "green tea bushes." Rather, it is the manufacture of the tea bush's glossy green leaves that determines whether the tea will be black, green, oolong, or white.

Black Tea

Recognized for its hearty, full-bodied flavor, black tea is the most popular tea in the Western world. In the United States, it accounts for over 90 percent of all tea consumed, often in the form of iced and ready-to-drink teas. However, with recent media focus on the high antioxidant content of green tea, health-conscious tea drinkers will likely turn the trend around as they seek out more green (and even white) teas in the future (see Chapter 5).

Tea Processing

Each category of tea—black, green, oolong, and white—is processed (prepared for packing and consumption) differently. Once the leaves are plucked from the fields, the process begins. Black tea, is the most processed tea type. It can undergo either the CTC or Orthodox processing method, which are explained below.

Both of the following methods begin with a step known as *withering*, in which freshly harvested leaves are spread out on tables or trays and left to air dry or "wither." This preserves the leaves by removing most of the moisture. As the moisture evaporates, the leaves become soft and limp in preparation for the next step. This step depends on which method is used:

CTC. (CUT, TEAR, CURL) METHOD. This processing method uses machines to literally cut, tear, and curl the withered tea leaves into small grainy pieces. The leaves are then fired (dried) to remove the remaining moisture. The CTC method provides quick processing for a high volume of tea leaves, as is commonly used in tea bags.

ORTHODOX METHOD. During this tea processing method, the withered leaves are rolled, oxidized (fermented), and then fired. These steps are further detailed:

• **Rolling.** Machines break the cells in the withered tea leaves, releasing their juices and enzymes. This exposes them to the air and enhances oxidation, which is the next step. In the highest quality tea, this rolling process is done by hand.

• **Oxidation.** Also known as *fermentation*, oxidation begins during the rolling process as the enzymes and juices of the broken leaves are exposed to air, resulting in a natural chemical process that produces the tea's unique aroma and flavor. The rolled leaves are spread out in a temperature- and humidity-controlled room where the tea leaf color deepens from green to a reddish-brown, and then to nearly black.

• **Firing.** The oxidized tea leaves are fired, or dried, through slow heating in a drying chamber. This stops the oxidation process and dehydrates the leaves in preparation for storage.

Green Tea

Green tea is not oxidized. Immediately after plucking and before rolling (see "Tea Processing" above), the tea leaves are steamed or pan-fired to prevent

According to the Tea Association of Canada, teenagers recognize the health benefits of many types of tea, drinking 41 percent, black; 24 percent, green; 48 percent, herbal infusions; and 80 percent, iced tea. Clearly, the numbers add up to teens drinking more than one type of tea.

oxidation by eliminating the leaf's enzymes. This also keeps the tea leaves green, which produces a light-colored liquor and a delicate, sometimes pungent or grassy taste.

Green teas are the most commonly consumed teas in Asia, but there was a time when they were equally popular in the United States. Prior to World War II, 40 percent of all tea consumed in America was green and 40 percent was black. Oolong was consumed by the remainng 20 percent. The advent of the war resulted in the loss of the tea trade with the East. Americans have been drinking mostly black tea ever since, a direction that may change as the trend towards tea focuses on its health benefits (see Chapter 5).

Oolong Tea

Partially oxidized anywhere from 10 to 70 percent, oolong ("Black Dragon") tea is a cross between black and green tea, sharing characteristics of both. Oolongs have a delicate orchid-like fragrance, but are more full-bodied than green tea and require a longer steeping time (see brewing chart on page 66). Since the mid-1800s, the island of Taiwan has been recognized for producing some of the world's finest oolongs.

Pouchong is the least processed oolong. In China, it is called green oolong and sometimes is mistakenly called green tea, which it is not, because it is slightly oxidized, about 10 to 20 percent. It has a milder flavor than oolong, but is stronger than green tea.

White Tea

White tea is the rarest and least processed tea. Harvested only once a year in the early spring, white tea is primarily from mainland China, where it is made from very young tea leaves or buds covered with tiny, silvery hairs. White tea is steamed and dried immediately after plucking to prevent oxidation, giving it a light, delicate taste. Recently, research has identified white tea as having more

Pu-erh

It is worth noting that there is a little-known tea, called pu-erh, which has a unique processing and aging formula that puts it in a category all its own. Named for a former tea-trading center in China's Yunnan province, pu-erh is both a black and green tea made from a large-leaf variety of Camellia sinensis called Dayeh.

Pu-erh tea is withered like black and green tea, then, while still moist, it is stacked into mounds. Watchful attendants continually turn the piles while Mother Nature's secret recipe slowly goes to work, using air temperature and the leaf's own bacteria, moisture, and size to create a highly prized tea with a strong, earthy flavor. The process can be likened to composting a pile of leaves.

The result is a tea that actually improves with age—some pu-erhs are fifty or more years old. It is a tea that is believed to have curative properties that lower cholesterol, aid digestion, and encourage weight loss.

disease-fighting antioxidants than black, green, or oolong tea (see Chapter 5), fueling its growing popularity and attracting other tea-growing regions to cultivate white tea.

Tea Blends

Blended teas are a mixture of tea leaves from different origins and of similar size that are brought together to create a specific flavor. Flowers, flavoring oils, or spices may also be added to the mix. Very few teas have the quality and character to stand alone as self-drinking teas, so most teas are blends. It's nothing new; teas have been blended for centuries, although not always for the benefit of the consumer. In the 1700s, before the British government repealed their outrageous tea taxes, unscrupulous tea traders mixed tea leaves with tree leaves, sawdust, and even gunpowder to increase their supply.

Today, a blend can be a tea company's signature. For example, Ruth Bigelow built one of America's most successful tea companies on a blend of black tea,

Hibiscus Flower

Who Is Earl Grey?

Earl Grey tea can be found just about anywhere tea is sold, but who exactly is Earl Grey? Earl was actually his title, not his name. Charles Grey (1764–1845) was England's 2nd Earl Grey. He was a political reformer and England's prime minister from 1830–1834. But his claim to fame is tea, not politics. It's said the tea that bears his name, a blend of black tea scented with the oil of bergamot, is a special recipe that was made for him by a Chinese mandarin when Grey was serving as a diplomat in China. Another story claims he was given the recipe while serving as prime minister. What is certain is Earl Grey has been one of the West's most popular tea blends for two centuries.

orange rind, and spices called "Constant Comment." Another tea company, Harney & Sons, has made a name for itself by blending teas for some of the most recognized companies in America. This practice is called private labeling, and Harney & Sons has created blends for Neiman Marcus; Williams-Sonoma; and the Ritz Carlton, Wyndham, Hyatt, and Four Seasons hotels.

While tea blending has become a skilled art for some, the technique actually developed as a way for tea merchants to achieve a consistent character of tea from season to season, creating customer loyalty for specific blends. English Breakfast, Irish Breakfast, and Russian Caravan are all popular black tea blends produced by many tea companies. But while the names are the same, the actual blend varies from brand to brand, and so will the taste.

Scented and Flavored Teas

Scented and flavored teas are dried with fruits or flowers or infused with aromatic oils of spices, fruits, flowers, or nuts. The process of scenting tea is said to have originated with jasmine tea during China's Sung Dynasty (960–1279 CE). Today, jasmine is the most popular scented tea in China. Jasmine blossoms at night, so in the evening, just prior to their opening, the freshly picked flowers are laid next to the dried tea leaves. When the blooms open, their fragrance is released and absorbed by the tea. The tea also absorbs the flower's moisture and must be re-fired (see page 45). The process is repeated as many as seven times. The more repetitions, the higher the grade of tea. Jasmine tea is usually prepared with green or oolong tea, but you can also purchase jasmine-scented black tea. For example, Jasmine Yunnan is a black tea from China's Yunnan province.

The most popular scented tea in the West is Earl Grey, a blend of black tea

Teaneck Tea

How much is a million? That is a question Ms. Ponchick's second grade class knows all about. When one of her students asked that very question, Ms. Ponchick, a teacher at Whittier School in Teaneck, New Jersey, decided to answer the question with tea. Actually, tea tags. She directed her class on a quest to collect and count one million tea bag tags. Along the way, she created a tea-centered curriculum and captured national media attention. *The New York Times* featured the Teaneck tea story in November 1988, followed the next month by a story in the *Wall Street Journal.* Then came the tea tags and letters from all over the world, as far away as Sydney, Australia and Kuala Lumpur, Malaysia!

For over two decades now, Ms. Ponchick and her classes have continued to collect tea tags and media attention. Their story has been mentioned in newspapers, magazines, and even books. She surpassed the million mark in June of 1992, but Ms. Ponchick's enthusiasm did not stop there. Now, she and her classes are on their way to discovering what a billion tea tags looks like!

In 1993, Ms. Ponchick and her class worked with master tea blender John Harney of Harney & Sons, Inc., to create Teaneck Tea, a mango-flavored black tea, which is available for sale. Profits from the sales are for purchasing books for the school library. To order the tea, call 1-888-HARNEYT. As Ms. Ponchick says, "It is the only tea created by second grade students, the only tea named after a town, and the only tea where the profits from tea sales go toward purchasing new books for a school library." This is really a perfect pairing, because nothing seems better suited for each other than a good book and a cup of tea.

Everything in Moderation

Can excessive tea consumption lead to temporary insanity? In July 2003, the Associated *Press* reported that tea drinking was the reason a Florida judge dismissed charges on a man accused of aggravated assault and burglary. Defense attorney Mike Hunter claimed his client, who had been drinking up to ten cups of jasmine tea a day to settle his stomach, was temporarily insane when he threw a brass duck through his neighbor's' glass door and chased her down the street with a dagger.

Three court-appointed psychologists reported that the accused had suffered from psychosis induced by jasmine tea. Hunter reported that a forensic toxicologist said jasmine can be hallucinogenic. Apparently his client had not been told to drink only one to two cups a day.

sprayed with oil pressed from bergamot oranges (*citrus bergamia*), a pear-shaped fruit grown in the Mediterranean and also used in perfume production. One of the most distinctive scented teas is Lapsang Souchong, a China black tea identified by its smoky scent and red liquor, obtained by smoking the leaves over pine needles during the drying process.

TERRIFIC TEAS

As adults, we enjoy indulging in our favorite specialty beverages, a category, which until recently, favored coffee connoisseurs with drinks like Frappuccinos and cappuccinos. Fortunately, now there are some terrific tea drinks that are gaining popularity and becoming increasingly easy to find. These delicious drinks include spicy rich chai, milky sweet bubble tea, and the unique kombucha culture with its ancient history and amazing health claims.

Chai

Chai means tea in many parts of the world, but in India it is something special.

Tea should be stored in a cool, dry place that is low in humidity and out of direct sunlight. Because tea absorbs surrounding odors, use an airtight container like a tin or a glass jar sealed with a gasket. Tea stored in this manner should stay fresh about six months.

Tea-Tasting Terms

Tea lovers often favor certain kinds of tea—some preferred potions may offer an early morning spice of energy, others may soothe the mind and body after a hectic day. You—or your coffee-loving friends—may be surprised to discover that an entire glossary of words has been developed to aid in the understanding of this seemingly simple, yet surprisingly complicated process, of discerning the quality of a cup of tea.

You may want to host your own tea-tasting party. Invite a few fellow tea lovers over to sample some cups and share their personal impressions of each elixir. It could be a formal affair in your dining room with fine china, or a casual gathering around your kitchen island, you set the mood—and the table!

Slurp, swish, and spit. Certainly not acceptable behavior for an afternoon tea party. Unless of course you're tasting, or cupping tea. To determine quality, taste, and color, tea cupping is used around the world. But you don't have to be a professional to appreciate the art of tasting tea; you can try it at home.

In addition to the tea leaves, all you'll need is a cupping spoon (a teaspoon will do), a cup of clean water, a sink or spittoon, and an identical six-ounce cup or bowl for each tea you'll be tasting. (To see the true color of the leaves, a white cup or bowl is best.)

Place different tea leaves in each container and pour boiling water over the leaves. Consistency is important, so use the same water for each tea, steeped for the prescribed amount of time. Like teas should use the same temperature of water steeped for the same amount of time.

First judge the quality of the liquor by its appearance. Use the spoon to scoop the wet tea leaves out of the container so you can sample their aroma and examine the leaves. Write down your impressions. Use the tea terms on page 52 as a guide.

Between each sampling, rinse the spoon in the cup of clean water. Next, taste the tea by spooning the liquor and sucking it into your mouth with a loud slurp. Slurping will simultaneously spray the tea over the taste buds on your tongue and the back of your mouth. Test the tea's astringency by swishing it around. Then spit the tea into a spittoon or sink and write down your impressions again. Keep your notes as a reference for future tea comparisons.

To start with, what is the difference between an infusion and a decoction? When you immerse your tea leaves in hot water and let them steep, or soak, to extract their flavor, the resulting brew, or liquor, is an infusion. A decoction is just the opposite. Instead of steeping the leaves, you extract the flavor by boiling them in the water. This is not recommended for tea leaves, but is used for some medicinal herbs.

A few of the more colorful established terms are included here, courtesy of the Tea Association of Canada. Most of these terms appear in "A Glossary of Tea" by the Tea Council.

TERMS DESCRIBING THE DRY TEA LEAF:

Black. A black appearance is desirable, preferably with "bloom."

Bloom. A sign of good manufacture and sorting (where reduction of leaf has taken place before firing). A "sheen" that has not been lost through over-handling or over-sorting.

Bold. Pieces of the leaf that are too large for the particular grade.

Chesty. Dry tea leaves with an unpleasant odor from wood in the tea chest or unseasoned packing materials.

Chunky. A very large- or broken-leaf tea.

Even. Teas true to their grade, consisting of pieces of leaf fairly even in size.

Flaky. Flat, open pieces of leaf often light in texture.

TERMS DESCRIBING THE INFUSED TEA LEAF:

Biscuity. A pleasant aroma often found in well-fired Assam tea.

Bright. A lively, bright appearance, which usually indicates the tea will produce a bright liquor.

Dark. A dark or dull color that usually indicates poorer leaf quality.

Green. When referring to black tea, it means the leaf has been under-fermented, or it can be a leaf plucked from immature bushes. It can also be caused by poor rolling during making or manufacture. This will often result in a raw or light liquor.

Tarry. A smoky aroma that should be present only in Lapsang Souchong tea.

TERMS DESCRIBING TEA LIQUOR:

Baggy. An unpleasant taste, normally resulting from the tea being carried or wrapped in unlined hessian bags.

Bakey. Tea liquor with an unpleasant taste caused by over-firing tea, resulting in the loss of too much moisture during the manufacture process.

Body. A liquor having both fullness and strength, as opposed to being thin.

Brassy. An unpleasant metallic [taste] quality similar to brass. Usually associated with unwithered tea.

Bright. A lively, bright liquor characteristic of a high quality tea.

Brisk. Good quality tea with a lively (not flat) taste.

Character. A desirable quality in a liquor that identifies where a tea is grown.

Coarse. A tea producing a harsh, undesirable liquor with taste to match.

Common. A very plain, light, and thin liquor with no distinct flavor.

Coppery. A good quality black tea with a desirably bright, coppery infusion.

Dull. Not clear, lacking any brightness or briskness.

Fruity. An overly ripe taste, which can result from over-fermenting during manufacture and/or bacterial infection before firing or drying.

Full. Strong tea without bitterness and with good color.

Gone Off. A flat or old tea. Often denotes a high moisture content.

Green. When referring to black tea liquor, it denotes an immature "raw" character. This is mostly due to under-fermenting and sometimes to under-withering during manufacture.

Hard. A very pungent liquor, a desirable quality in tea.

Harsh. A very rough taste generally due to the leaf being under-withered during manufacture.

Lacking. Describes a neutral liquor with no body or pronounced characteristics.

Light. Liquor lacking body and color.

Malty. Desirable characteristic in some Assam teas. A full, bright tea with a malty taste.

Mature. An intermediate taste that is neither bitter nor flat.

Muddy. Liquor with a dull, opaque appearance.

Muscatel. A grapey taste. Desirable character in Darjeeling teas.

Point. A liquor with desirable acidity and brightness.

Pungent. Astringent [sharp flavor], with a good combination of briskness, brightness, and strength.

Rasping. A very coarse and harsh liquor.

Raw. A bitter, unpleasant taste.

Soft. The opposite of brisk. Caused by inefficient fermentation and/or drying.

Stewed. A soft liquor having an undesirable taste and lacking point. Caused by faulty firing, or drying, at low temperatures, often with insufficient airflow through the oven during tea manufacture or making.

Strong. Liquor with a sharp, powerful character.

Thin. An insipid light liquor that lacks desirable characteristics.

Weedy. A grass or hay taste associated with teas that have been under-withered during manufacture and sometimes referred to as "woody."

India is the world's largest producer and consumer of tea, and that's no surprise when you learn the delicious way Indians have been preparing their chai for centuries. In India, chai is a sweet combination of milk, black tea, and spices, a preparation that is as much a daily staple as a cultural tradition.

While the mix varies from recipe to recipe, traditional chai is a combination of spices, which could include cloves, cinnamon, cardamom, star anise, peppercorn, ginger, and sometimes fennel or aniseed. The spices are ground and brewed in water with black tea, then strained and combined with milk and sweetener.

Fortunately, you don't have to search through your spice cabinet to create your own chai. Its growing popularity in the United States has taken chai tea from relative obscurity to grocery store shelves, where now you can buy chai loose leaf tea and tea bags, powder mixes, or liquid concentrate. Chai tea can be served as an iced beverage, but chai tea lattes are one of the hottest "new" drinks at coffeehouses across the country, where they offer a delicious alternative to coffee. Diehard coffee drinkers, who would never trade their cappuccino for a cup of tea, may be lured by chai's hearty, rich flavor. Add steamed milk with a dollop of whipped cream and the perfect crossover beverage is born.

American manufacturers of chai vary their spices, creating their own distinctive flavors. The leader in the industry, Oregon Chai, uses vanilla and honey to appeal to Americans' sweet tooth. With products on grocery shelves in all fifty states and Canada and double-digit annual growth, Oregon Chai is apparently on to something. Even Starbucks tried to buy Oregon Chai's recipe, but the proposal was turned down.

The chai tea market as a whole is experiencing tremendous growth. According to the *Tea Is "Hot" Report* produced by Seattle's Sage Group International, annual American sales of chai tea jumped from $24 million in 1999 to $69.7 million in 2002, with tremendous increases in sales predicted.

Vanilla Plant

Bubble Tea

Everyone will recognize the phrase "shaken, not stirred" as a kind of trademark of a certain British secret agent from the silver screen, but it's also a key part of the recipe for an increasingly popular milky sweet iced drink called bubble tea, also known as black pearl tea, tapioca tea, pearl milk tea, and boba tea (boba means "dominatrix of balls" in Mandarin and Cantonese, suggesting the image of large-breasted women).

Bubble tea basically consists of a green or black tea base mixed with milk or a cream-flavored powder and a sweetener of sugar, syrup, or sometimes honey. The ingredients are vigorously shaken with ice, like a martini, to create a head of frothy bubbles, hence the name bubble tea. Today the term bubble tea has come to refer to the gumball-sized black balls, or "pearls," of chewy tapioca that are often layered on the bottom of the milky sweet drink. Served in a clear cup or glass with an extra thick straw, the black balls (where the term "boba" comes from) create an eye-catching drink, sure to draw the curious.

Bubble tea originated in the 1980s in Taiwan, where it is sold on street corners. Its popularity is so widespread in Taiwan it has been dubbed the Taiwanese equivalent of India's chai. While bubble tea has not yet attained the level of chai tea's popularity in the United States, interest is growing at an amazing pace at teahouses across the country—and especially on the West Coast. According to the Sage Group International's *Tea Is "Hot" Report*, annual American sales of bubble tea increased six-fold from 1999 to 2002, growing from $5 million to $30 million.

Kissing is like drinking tea through a tea strainer; You're always thirsty afterwards.

—Old Chinese Saying

Kombucha

Kombucha is one of the newest and most unique tea drinks on the American market. Yet, despite its novelty in the West, kombucha has been a staple in Europe, Russia, and Asia, where its popularity reaches back thousands of years. The first written record of its use was in 221 BCE, during China's Tsing Dynasty, where it's described as "the remedy for immortality."

Kombucha is a natural culture of yeast and bacteria often compared to a sour-dough bread starter. A flat, rubbery pancake-like patty often called a "mushroom" or "mother," the kombucha culture is fermented with tea and sugar, transforming the tonic into natural acids that are said to detoxify the body. While there is no hard scientific evidence yet to validate their claims, loyal kombucha drinkers believe the mysterious brew provides a laundry list of health benefits that includes everything from preventing cancer and coronary disease, promoting effective kidney and liver function, relieving hot flashes and hemorrhoids, to even burning fat and eliminating baldness.

While such health claims sound too good to be true, there is one man who believes the tea has a chance to capture a portion of North America's $150 billion alternative beverage market. Stephen Lee, who helped start Stash Tea in the 1970s and Tazo Tea in the 1990s, was introduced to kombucha on a trip to Russia in the early 1990s. His company, Kombucha Wonder Drink (KWD), is the largest of a handful of commercial kombucha manufacturers in the United States. Distribution of KWD began in the fall of 2001 and it's now available at a growing list of restaurants, tea shops, and upscale grocery stores across the United States. Pasteurized for safety, KWD is made with green and oolong tea and sold in glass bottles as a ready-to-drink tea. Its unusual flavor is a bubbly balance between slightly sweet and mildly tart. Its biggest target market is baby boomers who are attracted to its healthful image and low sugar and caffeine content.

For the do-it-yourselfer, the kombucha culture is commercially grown and sold to individuals for home brewing. A quick internet search will uncover many companies, chat rooms, and informational sources on the subject. However, the Food and Drug Administration has warned that microbiological contamination may occur if the kombucha culture is not fermented in a sterile environment, so keep that in mind.

HERBAL TEA

**Camellia
sinensis**

Herbal tea is not "real" tea, meaning it is not made from the leaves of the *Camellia sinensis* plant. Instead, herbal infusions, or *tisanes* in French, are made with the leaves, flowers, roots, bark, berries, bulbs, and seeds of plants. There are an

Reading Tea Leaves

"Matrons, who toss the cup and see the grounds of fate in grounds of tea."
—Alexander Pope (1688–1744)

The art of reading tea leaves is centuries old. While it's highly respected in the East, its popularity was lost in the West with the advent of the tea bag. As the use of loose leaf tea increases, so do the opportunities to practice this ancient art. To see what your cup of tea has to say about the future, follow these simple steps:

1. Brew loose leaf tea in a pot and pour, unrestrained, into your cup.

2. Drink all but the last sip, leaving a teaspoon of tea and the leaves in your cup.

3. Swirl the tea and leaves three times counter clockwise.

4. Turn the cup over and place on the saucer. Wait for the tea to drain out.

5. Turn the cup right side up and examine the pattern of the leaves.

6. Leaves near the top deal with the near future, leaves on the bottom of the cup, the distant future. Leaves near the handle are said to relate to the home.

7. The formation of symbols in the leaves is used to tell the future. A few include:

Triangle—inheritance	Cow—prosperity
Ladder—promotion	Dog—a good friend
Star—good luck	Cat—treachery
Ring—marriage	Umbrella—shelter
Tree—success, happiness	

estimated 10,000 species of herbs in the world, and like tea, the use of herbals predates written history. Increasingly popular today, herbal infusions usually do not contain caffeine.

Functional Teas

Functional teas are also known as medicinal teas. They are herbal teas with a concentration of ingredients, often with vitamins and minerals added, that are said to provide a specific health benefit. For example, a functional tea may claim to aid in digestion or weight loss, alleviate nausea, calm nerves, increase energy, or encourage sleepiness. Some herbals, like peppermint or chamomile, are commonly enjoyed alone, while many other infusions combine two or more herbs and/or spices. Crossover blends combine black, green, and oolong tea with herbal ingredients.

Special Healing Teas

These herbal teas are unique in that each is extremely popular in its native country, and each claims to have distinctly unique curative properties. Rich in vitamins, minerals, and antioxidants, these teas have been receiving increased attention in North America.

Yerba Mate (Ilex paraguariensis)

A relative of the holly family, yerba mate is a traditional South American drink grown primarily in Argentina, Paraguay, Uruguay, and southern Brazil. The dried, ground yerba leaves are prepared in the mate, which is Spanish for gourd, and enjoyed hot. In Paraguay, the beverage is prepared cold, called tereré, and often drunk from a cup made of a hollowed out cow horn. The yerba leaves grow wild on trees in the South American rainforest, where about 500 million pounds are cultivated annually.

A strong, smoky tea, yerba mate is loaded with vitamins and minerals including vitamins A, B, C, E; iron; zinc; magnesium; calcium; potassium; sodium; manganese; and selenium.

Yerba mate also has caffeine. Some yerba mate proponents will tell you it's really mateine, described as a mild central nervous system stimulant with a chemical structure resembling caffeine, but without its side effects. However, tests conducted by independent chemists and scientists have concluded that yerba mate does contain actual caffeine, a rare ingredient in herbal tea, and a fact that is important to remember if you are trying to keep caffeine out of your diet.

Peppermint

Popular Ingredients in Herbal Teas

The following ingredients are often found in herbal tea concoctions. In addition to being quite flavorful with distinct aromas, many herbal teas provide natural health benefits.

Anise (Seed) 〰 *Pimpinella anisum*
An ancient herb native to the Mediterranean, anise seeds taste and smell like licorice and are often used as a flavoring for liqueurs and candy. In fact, licorice candy is more likely flavored with anise than made with real licorice. Anise is used to aid digestion and respiratory infections.

Star anise, *Illicum verum*, is a Chinese evergreen tree named for its fruit's star-like shape. Because of its low cost and potent licorice-like flavor, it is often used commercially to replace the more expensive aniseed oil.

Chamomile 〰 *Matricaria chamomilla* (German) or *Anthemis nobilis* (Roman)
There are two types of chamomile commonly used in tea, German chamomile and Roman chamomile. Both have comparable daisy-like blossoms and a sweet, apple-like scent. In fact, the name chamomile is taken from the Greek words meaning ground apple. Folklore claims that ancient Egyptians highly prized chamomile for its curative properties. It is still one of the most popular tea herbs in use today.

Chamomile soothes irritated skin and upset stomachs, and relieves heartburn and indigestion. It is also a mild relaxant, used to calm nerves and encourage sleepiness.

Ginger 〰 *Zingiber officinale*
The ginger root is a popular spice used as a flavoring for food and tea. Gingerbread cookies, for example, are a favorite sweet and spicy holiday treat. But ginger has an age-old reputation as a digestion aid. Ancient Chinese and Greeks started nibbling on ginger about 2,000 years ago to settle upset stomachs and quell motion sickness, which is one of its most recognized uses. Ginger is also an anti-inflammatory, recommended by some for arthritis and bursitis.

Hibiscus 〰 *Hibiscus sabdariffa*
The tangy, sweet taste of hibiscus flowers makes them a favorite ingredient for tea blends. With many natural acids including citric, oxalic, and malic, as well as vitamin C, calcium, niacin, riboflavin, and iron, hibiscus flowers make a healthy and flavorful brew.

Lemon (Peel & Juice) ✎ Citrus limon

The sweet, tart taste of lemons can pucker your lips, flavor your fish, and quench your thirst (as in lemonade). Lemon is an excellent source of vitamin C, thought to bolster the body's immune system. Sailors used lemons at least 300 years ago to prevent scurvy while at sea. Lemon is also a delicious flavoring ingredient in both herbal and real teas. I recently enjoyed a wonderful lemon-flavored black tea, a perfect combination for anyone who likes the taste of both milk and lemon in their tea, without worry of curdling.

Licorice Root ✎ Glycyrrhiza glabra

The next time you reach for a cough drop to quell a sore, scratchy throat or constant cough, you may very well find yourself sucking on a licorice-flavored lozenge. Fifty times sweeter than sugar, licorice's strong (overpowering for some), sweet taste is a common flavoring for medicine, candy, and herbal teas. A centuries-old cough remedy, licorice is also used to relieve constipation.

Orange (Peel & Blossom) ✎ Citrus sinensis

Wonderfully sweet, juicy oranges are an excellent flavoring for food and tea. Once called golden apples by the ancient Greeks, oranges are native to southeastern Asia. Spanish and Portuguese explorers brought the orange tree to America, where it has adapted well and become an important agricultural crop in the warm, sunny climates of Florida, California, Texas, and Arizona. Florida even named the orange blossom its state flower.

Peppermint ✎ Mentha piperita

Native to Europe, peppermint is a relatively new herb. Discovered just a little over 300 years ago, commercial cultivation began in England around the middle of the 1700s. Since then it has become a widely popular herb. Its refreshing menthol flavor adapts easily to hot or iced tea, in blends or alone. In addition to its wonderful flavor, peppermint is known to aid in digestion and soothe an upset stomach.

Raspberry ✎ Rubus idaeus

The incredibly delicious raspberry is the perfect example of food that tastes good and is good for you. Herbalists in Europe and North America have been using raspberry leaf tea for hundreds of years to help women. Many believe it strengthens the uterus and prepares the womb for childbirth. Dr. Andrew Weil, noted American physician and author of several books, reports on his website (www.drweil.com) that experts do not agree on the safety of raspberry leaf tea use during pregnancy and he advises pregnant women to consult their doctors. However, raspberry leaf tea can be helpful for menstrual cramps, morning sickness, motion sickness, and diarrhea.

Rose Petals 〜 Rosa spp.
For centuries, the rose has been a symbol of love and beauty, a universal appreciation that has not diminished. Want proof? Just ask any florist on Valentine's Day.

Today the rose is the world's favorite garden flower. In the United States alone, approximately 60 million rose plants are produced for commercial use every year; 20 million for cut flowers and 40 million for landscape and ornamental use. Roses are also popular in scented teas and calming herbal blends, making their delicate petals just as pleasing in a cup as a bouquet.

Rooibos (Aspalathus linearis)

Nicknamed "red tea" because of its lovely jewel tone infusion, rooibos is a South African tea made from an otherwise ordinary shrub-like bush. Caffeine free, rooibos tastes very similar to black tea, only smoother. You can steep it all day without bitterness. Rooibos is rich in the minerals iron, potassium, calcium, copper, zinc, manganese, sodium, fluoride, and magnesium, and it also packs a powerful dose of antioxidants—super oxide dimutase, in particular. Antioxidants are compounds that can attack the body's naturally occurring free radicals that damage cells. Rooibos's antispasmodic properties may help alleviate stomach and digestive problems. The proprietor at my local tea shop claims to drink rooibos tea every day to ease discomfort from diverticulitus. The key, she claims, is to bring the water to a hard boil and let it steep for 10 to 20 minutes. I follow her instructions to the T and brew a cup whenever I have an upset stomach.

Honey Bush (Cyclopia intermedia; Cyclopia subternata)

Honey bush is the slightly sweeter, smoother, and little-known cousin of rooibos. Also from South Africa, there are over twenty species, but only two are used in commercial production, *Cyclopia intermedia* and *Cyclopia subternata*. Named for its bright yellow flowers with a sweet honey aroma, honey bush is packed with vitamin C, potassium, calcium, and magnesium. The healthful brew also contains isoflavones and coumestans, which may help prevent cancerous tumors and osteoporosis. Like rooibos, honey bush is also used to aid digestion and both are used in South Africa to relieve colic in babies.

Kava (Piper methysicum)

In Polynesia, tea made from kava root has been drunk for hundreds of years.

Kava comes from the root of a South Pacific pepper plant. Extracts from the root are commonly available in health food stores in pill form for use as an antidepressant, stress reliever, and muscle relaxant. But it is most powerful when its roots are ground into a fine powder and mixed with water and drunk as a tea, a method practiced for centuries in Polynesia. The active ingredient is an alkaloid that is said to produce a soothing, slightly intoxicating effect on the nervous system. You can purchase kava powder and brew up your own batch at home, but be careful. Some people who have enjoyed a little too much kava brew have actually been ticketed for driving under the influence. It should also be noted that in March 2002, the U.S. Food and Drug Administration (FDA) issued a warning concerning the use of products containing kava. Although liver damage is rare, the FDA suggests "Persons who have liver disease or liver problems, or persons who are taking drug products that can affect the liver, should consult a physician before using kava-containing supplements."

HISTORY OF A PERFECT CUPPA: CENTURIES IN THE MAKING

Throughout tea's long history, it has been used as medicine, eaten as food, and even formed into bricks to exchange as money for barter. But its most pleasurable use, simply steeping the tea leaves in hot water and enjoying its soothing and satisfying liquor, didn't come into play until just a few hundred years ago. Over the centuries many methods of tea preparation have been employed to create the perfect cup of tea.

T'ang Dynasty (618–907 CE)

During China's T'ang Dynasty, northern and southern China were united after four hundred years of political and cultural division, creating a cosmopolitan empire of unmatched wealth and power. Religion and the arts flourished, fine porcelain was developed, and Chinese poet Lu Yu wrote the book *C'ha Ching* (*The Classic of Tea*). At this time, tea was prepared by steaming and crushing fresh tea leaves and shaping them into bricks, or cakes, which could be easily carried. Tea cakes were torn into pieces and added to boiling, sometimes salted, water. If that sounds unappealing, just imagine adding dates or onions to the mix, which they sometimes did.

Song Dynasty (960–1279 CE)

The Song Dynasty, also known as the Sung Dynasty, brought China to its economic, intellectual, and artistic peak. China became the world leader in ceramics

development and tea drinking was elevated to an art form. Tea tournaments were held to taste and critique new varieties of teas, and whipped tea became the desired method of preparation. To whip the tea, tea leaves were ground into a fine powder in a small stone mill. A bamboo whisk was used to whip the powder and hot water together into a thick, frothy, bright green tea called matcha. During this period, Japanese Buddhist monk Eisai returned from China as a Zen Master, bringing with him the new school of Buddhism, new tea seeds, and the matcha tea preparation, which is still used in the Japanese tea ceremony.

Yuan Dynasty (1279–1368 CE)

Kublai Khan, grandson of Ghenghis Khan, led the Mongol invaders who defeated the Song Dynasty in 1279. Khan took the Chinese name yuan, or "first" to establish the Yuan Dynasty. Ruling China for nearly 100 years, the Mongols ignored the finely developed Chinese style of the Song. It's said that the Chinese culture was nearly destroyed. Attention to tea was lost. Venetian traveler and author Marco Polo spent approximately seventeen years in China as a diplomat for Khan, and tea is not mentioned in his accounts of this time.

Ming Dynasty (1368–1644 CE)

When the Ming Dynasty ousted the Mongols in 1368, the cultural perspective returned to the Chinese. The final native-born dynasty in China's history, the Ming unified China and significantly advanced the Chinese arts. The Great Wall was built during the Ming Dynasty, Yixing teapots were created, and tea returned to favor with the ruling class. In fact, the Yixing teapots (made of clay from China's Yixing region—the only source of this unique clay) have played a key role in how we drink tea today. The finely crafted teapots, still in demand, were developed specifically for steeping loose leaf tea in hot water. The porous purple Yixing clay absorbs and improves the flavor and aroma of the tea, seasoning it with each infusion.

This loose leaf preparation found favor with the Ming emperor, creating a demand for the steeped tea—rather than the whipped tea, popular with the Song Dynasty. When the Europeans came along toward the end of the Ming Dynasty, tea became an important trade product throughout Asia and Europe. The steeping technique used during the Ming is how the Western world discovered tea, and is the popular method still used today.

The Ming emperor's loose leaf method of brewing tea is still used today.

CAFFEINE IN TEA

All tea made from the leaf of the *Camellia sinensis* plant contains caffeine. The amount of caffeine in a cup of tea varies considerably depending on the amount of dry tea used, leaf size, water temperature, and how long the tea steeps. Caffeine is water soluble, dissolving more quickly as the water temperature increases. So the hotter the tea water and the longer the leaves steep, the more caffeine will be released into the cup. But how much caffeine is in the tea leaf before it is even plucked is also affected by many factors, including the elevation and age of the leaf, minerals in the soil, growth rate of the tea plant, and its manufacture. For example, the longer the oxidation/fermentation process during the manufacture of the tea leaf, the higher the caffeine content. Use the brewing information and chart below as a guideline for determining the amount of caffeine in your cup of tea.

You can purchase decaffeinated tea in which ethyl acetate or carbon dioxide processes are used to chemically remove caffeine; however a small amount of caffeine will remain. If you'd rather refrain from chemical treatments, there is a simple method to significantly decaffeinate tea during the brewing process. Up to 80 percent of caffeine is extracted from the tea leaves within the first minute of steeping. If you discard the first infusion after one minute and resteep the tea leaves, you can enjoy your tea with a lot less caffeine in your cup. However, if you are trying to avoid caffeine completely, you may want to consider an herbal infusion.

Tea has more than twice as much caffeine per pound than coffee, but because a pound of tea makes 200 cups, and a pound of coffee makes about 40 to 60 cups, the actual amount of caffeine in your cup is much less with tea than coffee.

Brewing Tea

Tea experts advise using two grams of tea, or approximately one teaspoon, for every 5.5 to 6 ounces of water. Because tea-leaf size varies, a teaspoon may not equal two grams of tea. For the perfect cup of tea a scale is recommended, as are the following instructions.

1. Use fresh, clean, cold water.

2. Heat the water as follows:

   - Bring water to a rolling boil for black tea. Don't over-boil, since it depletes the oxygen and results in flat-tasting tea.

   - Stop just short of a rolling boil for oolong tea.

   - The more delicate green and white teas require less heat. Bring water to a pre-boil, or just when air bubbles start to form.

3. Preheat the teapot (or teacup for single serving) with hot water. Discard before adding the tea leaves and heated tea water.

4. Pour the heated water over the tea leaves to infuse. Follow the general guidelines chart below for steeping time.

5. Depending on your steeping method, remove the infuser or use a strainer for the tea leaves.

Caffeine and Steeping Time

Gongfu, which is Chinese for "skill and practice," describes a formal tea brewing method dating back to China's Ming dynasty (1368–1644 CE) characterized by several short infusions using lots of tea leaves in small, fist-sized clay teapots and tiny teacups.

The following chart provides a guide to general steeping times for different types of tea, as well as the approximate amount of caffeine per cup, based on the suggested steeping times. It's also important to remember that the longer you steep your tea, the greater the caffeine content in your cup.

Types of Tea	Steeping Time	Approx. Caffeine Per Cup
Black	3–5 minutes	25–110 mg
Green	1–3 minutes	8–30 mg
Oolong	3–7 minutes	12–55 mg
White	1–8 minutes*	6–25 mg
Herbal	5–7 minutes	0 mg

*Instructions for steeping white tea vary widely. Ask your tea retailer for recommendations for the specific tea you purchase.

These are very general guidelines. Experiment with steeping times for your personal taste.

A Quick Fix

New technology has made it possible to brew a quality cup of tea in just a few seconds. The tea industry has not seen much innovation in the quick-fix category for hot tea since the creation of the tea bag in the early 1900s, but even a tea bag requires steeping time. Now a company has invented a way to brew whole-leaf tea in thirty seconds. Seattle-based Affinitea Brewing Technologies has developed an espresso-like machine that brews hot and iced tea, adjusting water temperature and pressure to the size of the tea leaf. Sold to retail tea outlets, company president Anthony Priley claims he is not trying to replace traditional tea brewing methods; rather, he is attempting to appeal to an entire segment of non-tea drinkers who would otherwise never take the time to brew a cup of tea.

Hopefully, after reading this chapter you've been inspired to visit your local tea shop and try a tea you've never had before. There is literally a world of teas for you to experiment with, and with nearly 3,000 varieties of tea available, it would take over eight years to try a new one every day! In the next chapter, you'll find even more inspiration as we discover where in the world tea comes from and how really good tea is grown.

CHAPTER 4

Teasof theWorld

Mother Nature's original tea garden was located in the monsoon district of southeastern Asia. . . . Before any thought was given to dividing this land into separate states, it consisted of one primeval tea garden where the conditions of soil, climate, and rainfall were happily combined to promote the natural propagation of tea.

—WILLIAM H. UKERS, *ALL ABOUT TEA*

The commercially cultivated *Camellia sinensis* bush spends its entire life pleasing others. Perpetually pruned, plucked, and processed, the pleasure is all ours. We immerse its leaf in scalding hot water, in the flavor-releasing process called the "agony of the leaves," and never allow it to experience what Mother Nature intended. Untouched by human, the tea bush would flower and grow into a tree; its limbs would toughen and reach upwards fifty or more feet high. But for harvesting convenience and quality in the cup, the tea bush is forever trimmed to a mere three to four feet.

While originally found in China, Tibet, and northern India, man has spread the seeds of *Camellia sinensis* and compelled it to take up roots all over the world. The tea plant has obliged. With proper care and feeding, it has rewarded its handlers by thriving in soil that had never nourished it before. From hot and humid tropical plantations to the cool, wet Pacific Northwest, the widespread cultivation of *Camellia sinensis* has been a challenging task, but after much toil and many trials, tea is now grown in over thirty countries around the world.

HOW DOES THE TEA GARDEN GROW?

Canadians have been drinking tea since the British Hudson's Bay Company first imported it in 1716.

The European traders first discovered tea as a beverage, not a plant. The laborious leaf processing was complete and all that was left to do was prepare a pot of hot water and enjoy. In fact, China kept the method of manufacture a secret from the West. Forbidden to observe the process for decades, botanists thought green and black tea were derived from two different tea plants, the viridis (green) and the bohea (black). It was nearly the middle of the nineteenth century, almost 250 years since the first chest of tea leaves crossed the South China Sea, before the plant-hunting Scotsman, Robert Fortune, settled the matter.

Western Tea's Fortune

After being defeated by Britain in the Opium Wars, China signed the Treaty of Nanking in 1842, opening up the country to additional trade and travel. This prompted the Horticultural Society of London to send a plant-collection expedition to China. Robert Fortune, superintendent of the Society's hothouses at its gardens in Chiswick, London, led the excursion, reaching China in the summer of 1843. Fortune attempted to blend in as a Chinese laborer by shaving his head and wearing native dress, but he was often surrounded by curious locals. Nevertheless, Fortune was able to observe growing methods and collect many plant species, including tea, which were sent back to London for cultivation and study. Over the years, Fortune returned to China several times, but on two occasions it was specifically for tea.

After tea was discovered growing wild in India, Britain realized their Indian empire offered conditions well suited for cultivating the profitable plant. Believing the long-cultivated China seeds would be superior to the wild Indian tea plants, Fortune was sent to China in 1848 to bring back seeds, plantings, and knowledgeable workers to jump-start the Indian tea industry. Fortune's expedition was very successful; ultimately, however, the China plants were not (see Chapter 2).

In 1858, the United States government thought tea would be a valuable agricultural product for the Southern states, so they hired Fortune to bring China tea seeds to the American South. Although tea bushes were grown in several states including Tennessee, Florida, Georgia, Louisiana, and the Carolinas, none ever achieved commercial success. Tea production is very labor-intensive, requiring approximately one worker per acre. It was thought the American attempts failed due to the high labor costs. It would take 100 years before technology provided an answer, and enabled another attempt at commercial tea production in the South. We'll take a closer look at this later in this chapter.

Thanks to the work of Robert Fortune, the West learned how to grow tea, but where to grow it was another matter. Around the world, there are an estimated six million acres dedicated to growing tea, which annually yield as much as 6.5 billion pounds of tea leaves. Much of the world's tea is grown on large estates, or plantations, also called "gardens." Often containing hundreds of hectares (one hectare equals 2.471 acres of land), tea gardens are independent operations providing the workers and their families with housing, schools, places of worship, and medical care.

Tea cultivation is often compared to wine because the essential elements of climate, soil, elevation, and manufacturing methods together create a multitude of flavor variations in a tea leaf, just as they do in a wine grape. Also like wines, teas are often named for the areas where they are grown—areas recognized for a particular flavor and character. Unlike wine, however, tea does not improve with age. An exception to this rule is China's pu-erh tea, which is processed using microbiological fermentation that allows it to age slowly.

Tea and Wine

According to John Vendeland, an agricultural consultant and Pacific Northwest tea grower:

Tea is also one of the world's most complex beverage crops, rivaling wine in the range of appearance and flavor characteristics that can be produced. To a great extent, this complexity results from the interaction of horticultural and processing factors.

Sun, Shade, and Soil

Shade trees protect the tea plants from the searing sun.

Camellia sinensis is a very hardy plant with a remarkably productive life span—with proper care, about 100 years. But despite its tough character, it does play favorites, preferring the hot and humid subtropical and tropical climates, aptly named the Torrid Zone, where temperatures can climb toward 100° F and where Mother Nature can easily match each digit on the thermometer with inches of annual rainfall. All that sun and rain can be troublesome for many living things, and *Camellia sinensis* is no different. Too much rain will rot its roots, so it prefers acidic soil with good drainage and just the right amount of shade. To protect its leaves from the searing sun, shade trees may be planted just for that purpose. The tea bush also has a comfort zone, experiencing its most prolific growth in temperatures that do not exceed 85° F. In fact, the best teas grow in cooler temperatures.

So how do you balance the tea plant's penchant for a tropical climate and cooler temperatures? Altitude is the answer. The higher the elevation, the cooler the temperature. The cooler temperatures slow the tea leaf growth, producing a tea with concentrated flavor and fully developed characteristics. Some of the world's finest teas are grown at elevations of 3,000 to 6,000 feet. One of the best examples of this process is Darjeeling tea. Often called the "champagne" of teas, Darjeeling tea is grown in India on estates upward of 6,000 feet.

In the wild, tea plants reproduce by cross pollination. This means that each plant is pollinated by another, resulting in a hit-or-miss approach to tea cultivation. Commercial tea growers cannot afford to chance the quality of their tea crop, so they've taken a much more selective approach to the process that goes right to the root of the problem—literally.

The commercial tea bush begins its long, carefully cultivated life as a seedling or a clone. Seeds are coddled in a nursery for about nine months until the new plants are ready for the field. While this is the less expensive method, it also tends to produce a lower yield and cup quality. Vegetative, or clonal propagation, is the predominant method of reproduction used today. A clone is created in the nursery using rooted cuttings from a mature leaf and axillary bud, then planted in the garden, producing a higher yield and allowing for better quality control. From level fields to mountain slopes, as many as 3,000 to 4,000 tea bushes per acre carpet the contour of the land and cover the earth in a lush green blanket. After about three to five years, depending on the elevation, the tea plant is ready for its first picking.

There is a great deal of poetry and fine sentiment in a chest of tea.

—Ralph Waldo Emerson (1803–1882)

A Bud and Two Leaves

There is an ancient story of a rare tea enjoyed exclusively by a Chinese emperor and his court. This tea was inaccessible to man; it could only be found growing wild in a remote mountainous area of China's Yunnan province. The only way to procure the desired leaves for the emperor's tea was to provoke a pack of mountain-dwelling monkeys who, when adequately agitated, would rip apart the tea trees and throw them at their antagonists below. The emperor's agents harvested the legendary monkey tea by plucking the leaves from the fallen limbs.

Fortunately, today the world does not rely on a band of angry monkeys to enjoy really good tea, although it is true that plucking good tea leaves is crucial to the quality of tea in the cup. Usually women, and sometimes machines, are entrusted for this important task. When Lu Yu wrote *The Classic of Tea* in the eighth century, harvesting tea leaves was taken very seriously—as the following passage from the book explains:

> Pickers were always women and usually girls. For three weeks before the picking they were required to abstain from eating fish and certain meats so that their breath may not affect the bouquet of the leaves. For the same reason the picker was to bathe every morning before setting out.

Much more important, of course, are the leaves themselves. The tender new leaves on a tea bush are called a *flush*. For good quality tea, the top two leaves and unopened bud are plucked. For fine tea, only the top leaf and bud are selected. The further down the tea bush the leaves are plucked, the lower, or coarser, the quality of the tea. Tea pluckers skillfully pinch the tips of the waist-high tea branches, gathering the first inch of growth and tossing it into baskets carried on their backs. Experienced workers can pluck about 30,000 shoots a day. A tea bush may produce over 1,000 leaves a year, and it takes about 2,000 to 3,000 leaves to make one pound of processed tea.

Tea is a treasure of the world.

—William H. Ukers,
All About Tea

With each plucking, new growth is stimulated. The number of flushes in a single year is dependent upon the climate. In tropical climates, a plant can flush every seven to ten days throughout the year. In cooler, mountainous areas, the number of flushes is seasonal. For example, India's Darjeeling tea is harvested from spring to fall and identified as first flush (March/April), second flush (May/June), and autumnal flush (timing depends on the rainy season).

MAKING THE GRADE

Once plucked and processed by either the orthodox or the CTC (Cut, Tear, Curl) method explained in Chapter 3, a mechanical sifter with mesh screens is used to separate the tea by grades, which are determined by leaf size, not flavor. This step ensures the same size tea leaves will be packaged together.

Black Teas

Black teas of India, Ceylon (Sri Lanka), Java, Sumatra, Africa, a few Chinese teas, and a handful of other black teas are distinguished by a number of different grade descriptions. These terms differ when describing whole-leaf tea and broken-leaf tea. You'll never look at black tea the same again!

Grade Descriptions for Whole-Leaf Tea

OP - Orange Pekoe. Pekoe (pronounced *pee-koh*) is derived from the Chinese words *bai hoa,* meaning "white down," referring to the fine white hairs on the young leaf bud. Pekoe is a distinction indicating whole-leaf tea. The "tip" of a tea plant refers to the golden or silver tips of the unopened bud found on the end of the tea branch. Orange Pekoe is a whole-leaf tea with few or no tips.

FOP - Flowery Orange Pekoe. Flowery Orange Pekoe is a whole leaf containing more tips.

GFOP - Golden Flowery Orange Pekoe. A higher grade than Flowery Orange Pekoe, Golden Flowery Orange Pekoe has more tips.

TGFOP - Tippy Golden Flowery Orange Pekoe. A fine, high-quality tea that has many tips and is called "tippy." Tippy Golden Flowery Orange Pekoe is a whole-leaf tea with a larger proportion of golden tips than Golden Flowery Orange Pekoe. Finest Tippy Golden Flowery Orange Pekoe (FTGFOP) is tea of exceptional quality. Special Finest Tippy Golden Flowery Orange Pekoe (SFTGFOP) would be an even finer tea, with a large number of tips.

The numbers 1 or 2 may be added after the leaf grade designation to further indicate top-quality tea. For example, Assam SFTGFOP1 would be a superior Indian black tea. Also, when the name of an estate is added, it indicates where the tea leaves were grown, and to add the distinction of "vintage" means the leaves are from one harvest and have not been blended with another. For example, Chamong Estate Vintage 1st Flush is a superior black tea from the season's first harvest at the Chamong tea plantation located in the Rong Bong Valley of Darjeeling.

Grade Descriptions for Broken-Leaf Tea

BOP - Broken Orange Pekoe. Broken Orange Pekoe is made up of broken or small tea leaves. Just as in the whole-leaf tea grades mentioned above, Broken Orange Pekoe can be described as Golden, Flowery, and/or Tippy. Broken leaves have a greater total surface area than whole-leaf tea, allowing them to infuse faster.

Fannings. Smaller than Broken Orange Pekoe, fannings are little, grainy tea leaf fragments commonly used in tea bags.

Dust. Used in tea bags, dust is the smallest tea-leaf particle.

Green Teas

A green tea farm.

Most of the world's green and oolong teas come from China, Japan, and Taiwan, where the standard grades used in black tea do not apply. Each country has its own unique, and sometimes complicated, way to define the tea leaf. With green China tea, the age and style of the leaf are what's important, and within the categories listed on the next page there are additional grade levels. For example, Pinhead to Pea Leaf are distinctions for Gunpowder tea, which are additionally

Are There Oranges in Orange Pekoe?

What is the orange in Orange Pekoe? Many people mistake it for a flavoring or color. It is neither. Surprisingly, there is a royal reason behind the misunderstood label. The Dutch royal family, the House of Orange, received the fine China tea from the early Dutch traders. Referring to tea as Orange Pekoe was like stamping a seal of royal distinction on the exotic new beverage. Unfortunately, the name has become too familiar and is often incorrectly applied to tea of inferior quality.

subdivided by quality into Extra First Pinhead, Pinhead, Pea Leaf, first, second, third, fourth, fifth, sixth, seventh, and Common Gunpowder.

Grade Descriptions for Chinese Green Teas

Gunpowder. Named gunpowder because the young tea leaves are tightly rolled into little pellet-shaped green balls resembling gunpowder.

Imperial. Loosely rolled pellets formed from older tea leaves sorted out of gunpowder.

Young Hyson. Hyson is Chinese for "bright spring." Young Hyson is a high-quality tea leaf picked in the early spring and rolled long and thin.

Hyson. An old leaf rolled to look like a combination of Young Hyson and Imperial.

Twankay. Poor quality, unrolled old leaf.

Hyson Skin and Dust. Hyson Skin is a lower-quality leaf than Twankay, and Dust is the lowest-quality grade of China green tea leaf.

Most of the world's green teas come from China, Japan, and Taiwan.

Grade Descriptions for Japanese Green Teas

Gyokuro. Japanese for "pearl dew," Gyokuro is a high-quality grade of tea grown in the shade and hand rolled from tender new buds of the season's first flush.

Tencha. Made from the same buds as Gyokuro, Tencha is naturally dried, flat tea leaves which are used in the Japanese tea ceremony. The leaves are ground into a fine powder and whisked into a bright green frothy tea called matcha.

Sencha. Japanese for "common," Sencha is the most popular tea in Japan. But common does not mean poor quality. There are many high-quality Sencha teas, depending on the manufacturing process (steamed, pan-fired, basket-fired, etc.) and where the tea is grown.

Bancha. Japanese for "last tea," Bancha is the lowest-quality Japanese tea made from coarse leaves pruned from the plant at the end of the season.

Oolong Teas

The highest quality and quantity of oolong teas come from China's Fujian province and the island of Taiwan, which is opposite mainland China directly across the Taiwan Strait. Unlike black and green teas, oolongs are graded on the quality of the liquor produced by steeping the leaves. There are many different distinctions from Standard (poorest quality) to Choice, Choicest, Fancy, Fanciest or Extra Fancy (best quality). The finest oolong grades are Fancy, Fanciest, or Extra Fancy. For example, Fancy Formosa Silver Tip Oolong would be a high-quality oolong tea from Taiwan.

THE WORLD'S FINEST TEAS

Some of the world's finest teas are produced in China, Taiwan, Japan, India, and Sri Lanka, where the perfect blend of climate and care come together in a cup of tea. From ancient China to modern times, centuries have passed between the initial propagation of the tea plant to the present-day cultivation. But the number of years a country has cultivated tea does not seem to be important in the quality of leaf it produces for the pleasure of all.

China

China has been cultivating *Camellia sinensis* for thousands of years. Legends tell us this is where it all began; from the delightful discovery of Emperor Shen Nong to the meditation of Bodhidharma and the wisdom of Lu Yu, the legacy of the leaf has its roots in the soil and the stories of this ancient land.

A vast country of great natural diversity, within China's nearly 3.7 million square miles, black, green, oolong, white, and pu-erh teas are manufactured. Each category of tea has its finest examples, often with poetic names like *Iron Goddess, Little Red Robe,* or *Phoenix Bird,* and comes from regions known for the processing of a particular variety of tea.

China's best-known green tea, *Lung Ching* (Dragon Well), is grown in the West Lake region of Hangzchou, the home of China's National Tea Museum and not far from Shanghai in eastern China. Well-known author James Norwood Pratt describes Dragon Well, one of China's most celebrated teas, in the first edition of his wonderful book *Tea Lover's Treasury,* as "ethereally complex with a haunting, distant sweetness. No wonder it's China's most famous green tea. You could drink it all day long."

China black tea is separated into North China (black leaf) and South China (red leaf) Congou. Congou is a standard trade name for China black tea. Keemun is the most famous North China Congou. Grown in the Anhui province in eastern China, Keemun had been an undistinguished green tea until the nineteenth century, when the manufacture of black tea was attempted and this fine tea was discovered.

Well-known South China Congou teas Paklum, Panyong, Pakling, and Padrae are grown in the Fujian province on China's southeast coast. This is also where the distinctively smoky Lapsang Souchong tea is produced. Other well-known China Congou teas are Ningzhou, from south China's Jiangxi province, and Yichang, from the Hubei province in central China. The Fujian province is also the source of China's rare white and popular oolong teas. The partially oxidized oolong tea is said to have originated here.

The story is told of a man named Wu Liang who was preparing green tea from freshly plucked mountain leaves but became distracted during the process. By the time he returned, the tea had begun to oxidize. He fired it immediately to stop the process and found the resulting brew delicious. *Ti Kuan Yin* (Iron Goddess of Mercy) is one of the finest examples of China oolong tea.

The southern province of Yunnan, a mountainous region bordering Vietnam, Laos, and Burma, is known for its black and pu-erh tea.

Taiwan

Taiwan produces green, and some black, teas but is famous for its oolongs. As the country was formerly known as Formosa (Portuguese for "beautiful"), teas from Taiwan still carry the Formosa name. The island is separated from mainland China by the 115-mile-wide Taiwan Strait connecting the East and South China Seas, which was navigated for centuries by European tea traders.

The first tea plants were brought to Taiwan from their native China in the mid-1800s by migrating mainland Chinese, specifically from the Fujian Province directly opposite Taiwan, and as mentioned, a region known for its oolong tea. At first, the immigrants may have tried duplicating the China oolong, but the island provided an ideal combination of natural elements that resulted in a tea many

Pouchong, the least fermented oolong tea, is grown in Taiwan's Pinglin region, located about an hour outside of Taipei. This is also home to the multi-million dollar Pinglin Tea Industry Museum, reputed to be the world's largest tea museum.

believe superior to China's. Grown near Taipei on the island's north end at about 1,000 feet above sea level, the tea leaves manufactured into Formosa oolong are plucked from April to December.

Japan

Taking tea in Japan is an integral element of a culture that has elevated drinking tea to a spiritual art form known the world over as the Japanese tea ceremony, or *chanoyu*. That the simple art of drinking tea could be raised to such an exalted level seems a mystery until one realizes the first tea seeds and method of preparation were introduced to Japan by Buddhist monks returning from travels in China in the eighth century.

Tea is grown throughout Japan from May through October. While the great percentage of it is processed as green tea, very little is exported since nearly all of the tea is consumed at home. In fact, to meet their seemingly unquenchable thirst for tea, the Japanese must import it. They are one of Taiwan's biggest tea-buying customers.

India

India has only endeavored to manufacture *Camellia sinensis* since the first chests of Assam tea were auctioned in London in 1839. It took a few years to get the kinks out of the system and recognize the native plants were preferred over the imported Chinese plants, but when it was finally settled propagation of the plant was a phenomenal success. Manufactured into mostly black tea, today India is the world's largest producer and consumer of tea, producing 826.2 million kilograms of tea in 2002. The tea industry is also India's second largest employer, providing jobs for over one million workers (more than 50 percent women). Three of India's tea-producing regions are home to some of the world's finest teas. These regions include Assam, Darjeeling (the tea from which, as previously mentioned, is often referred to as the "champagne" of teas), and the Nilgiri Hills.

Assam

Tea plants were first found growing wild in the forests of Assam in the 1820s. Their discovery eventually sparked the development of the Indian tea industry. Since then, Assam, located in the Brahmaputra Valley in India's far northeast corner, has become the largest tea growing area in the world, accounting for about half of India's annual tea production.

Darjeeling

Located at the tip of northeastern India, next to Nepal, Darjeeling has been a well-known hill resort since the British army sent troops there on holiday in the mid-1800s. Tucked in the foothills of the Himalayan range, it is a striking region with extraordinary mountain vistas—including Mount Everest, which at 29,028 feet is the world's tallest peak. Surrounding tea plantations extend from 2,500 to 6,500 feet, producing one of the world's greatest teas.

Nilgiri Hills

Located on India's southern tip, the Nilgiri Hills (translated "Blue Mountains") sit in the shadow of the Eastern and Western Ghat Mountains, framed by the Bay of Bengal and the Arabian Sea. The thick jungles, abundant waterways, rolling grasslands, and rugged mountains form a lush landscape that stretches into the Indian Ocean, almost as if reaching for the neighboring island of Sri Lanka. While Assam and Darjeeling have a seasonal spring-to-fall tea harvest, Nilgiri's more tropical climate allows for year-round plucking of tea bushes, which are grown at elevations of 100 to over 6,500 feet.

Sri Lanka

Just thirty miles off the southern tip of India, the teardrop-shaped island of Sri Lanka is nearly the size of Ireland. A fitting comparison since the Irish drink the most tea per capita, and tea is Sri Lanka's most important industry and largest employer, providing jobs for over one million people. The third largest tea-producing country in the world, Sri Lanka's tea industry generates hundreds of

millions of dollars in annual revenue—a big accomplishment for a relatively small country that didn't start growing tea commercially until the late 1800s. In the early 1800s, coffee was the island's biggest export product, which lasted until about 1875 when a widespread fungus wiped out the coffee plantations. Fortunately, an employee at a large coffee plantation, a Scotsman named James Taylor, had been experimenting with tea plants for several years prior to the devastating blight. His success was the perfect example and soon all the coffee plantations were replaced with tea, a task that was aided considerably when another Scotsman, Thomas Lipton, arrived in 1890. Sri Lanka's Tea Museum, near the central city of Kandy, showcases the country's early tea industry and has machinery on display that dates back more than a century.

Worker picking tea in Ceylon (now Sri Lanka), c. 1900.

Sri Lanka, formerly known as Ceylon, is home to some of the world's most desirable teas. Mostly black, all still carry the Ceylon name and are grown in the mountainous central and southern areas of the island and categorized by elevation into low-grown (up to 2,000 feet), medium-grown (2,000–4,000 feet), and high-grown (over 4,000 feet). The finest teas come from the high regions of Uva, Dimbula, and Nuwara Eliyah, where tea bushes grow at elevations up to 7,000 feet.

Tea, Please

It was December 24, 2003, when the ancient city of Bam, Iran, crumbled under the shock of a massive earthquake, killing over 30,000 people. Thousands more struggled with the loss of their homes, electricity, and running water. When more than a week later, the prospect of finding any survivors seemed hopeless, rescue workers discovered a hand rising from the rubble. Encouraged by hearing a weak plea for help, they toiled for several hours to pull 97-year-old Shahr-Banu Mazandarani from the debris. Frail after eight days of being buried alive without food or water, Ms. Mazandarani credited God for her survival. Then she asked for one thing—a cup of chai.

Africa and Indonesia

Tea is produced in many other countries. From Vietnam to Iran, Russia to Argentina, and Turkey to Tanzania, tea is grown on small, privately owned patches of land to large corporate-controlled plantations. Two areas of the world that produce tea in great quantity are Africa and Indonesia. In fact, both are on the world's top-five list of tea-producing countries. Most of this is black tea manufactured in the CTC (Cut, Tear, Curl) method, and is destined to be blended in a tea bag, often with teas from India and Sri Lanka.

The equator cuts through the middle of the massive continent of Africa, creating an ideal climate to grow tea—something many African countries do very well, including Burundi, Cameroon, Kenya, Madagascar, Malawi, Mozambique, South Africa, Rwanda, Tanzania, Uganda, Zaire, and Zimbabwe. The first tea grown outside Asia was in East Africa, where commercial cultivation began in the country of Malawi in the 1880s. It remains a major export crop in Malawi, but the country that produces the most tea in Africa is Kenya. Situated directly on the equator, the fertile highlands of southwest Kenya, near Lake Victoria, receive the perfect combination of climate, altitude, and ample rainfall. Here, tea is grown year round at elevations up to 7,000 feet.

Situated directly on the equator, the fertile highlands of Kenya offer perfect tea-growing conditions.

The Dutch East India Company set up shop in Indonesia during the infancy of the tea industry in the early seventeenth century. From its base on the island of Java, it initially traded for tea with Amoy (Xiamen) merchants from China's Fujian province. Little did the company know that 100 years later, Java would be at the center of Indonesia's own tea industry. Sitting squarely on the equator, Indonesia's chain of islands extends from the Indian to the Pacific Oceans in a tropical zone that puts Indonesia on the tea-growing map. After 200 years of success, much of Indonesia's tea industry was devastated during World War II, and the tea plantations took many years to recover. But with a lot of hard work, they bounced back, and today, Indonesia is one of the most successful tea-growing countries in the world.

Some of the island's best tea is grown at elevations of 400 to 6,000 feet on the

Despite the fact people usually think "coffee" when they hear the word "java," the majority of Indonesia's tea is grown on the island of Java.

Pengalengan Plateau, not far from Jakarta. The neighboring island of Sumatra is responsible for about a quarter of Indonesia's annual production, where at elevations of 800 to 2,400 feet, much of the tea is cultivated in the area of Pematangsiantar. Both green and black teas are produced year round. The black tea is exported, but much of the green tea is used domestically for jasmine-scented tea.

United States

In the United States, tea gardens are being cultivated in the unlikely locale of the Pacific Northwest. Rain clouds frequently roll in off the Pacific Ocean and across the Cascade Mountain Range, pausing over the Pacific Northwest like a thick blanket hanging low in the sky, blocking out the warm sunrays for weeks at a time. These cool, gray days aren't exactly the textbook formula for tea growing,

Hot Water from Iced Tea

Former President Bill Clinton got himself in hot water for holding fund-raising coffee klatches in the White House. And in 1996, Vice President Al Gore and the Democratic National Committee were steeped in a fund-raising controversy in which Gore used tea drinking as an excuse in his defense.

The controversy stemmed from a November 1995 meeting, where it was alleged that Gore agreed to make fund-raising phone calls from the White House. In a 1997 FBI investigative interview, Gore denied the phone calls were discussed at the November meeting.

But just ten months later, when handwritten notes from that very meeting surfaced and Gore appeared to be quoted talking about the fund-raising phone calls, he changed his story. He no longer denied the conversation took place; instead, Gore said he wasn't in the room. Blaming his bladder, Gore claimed he had drunk a lot of iced tea, and when the fund-raising calls were discussed, he must have been in the bathroom.

Classic American Technology

In the past, high labor costs made it impossible for commercial tea production to succeed in the United States. However, Mack Fleming's invention changed all that. He designed an air conveyance harvester that could do the work of 500 tea pickers.

Basically Fleming's invention is a mechanical tea picker that is a cross between a tobacco harvester and a cotton picker. Its success in the field has enabled American Classic Tea to compete in the tea market. Since it's introduction in 1987, American Classic Tea has fittingly been adopted as the official White House tea. American Classic Tea produces black tea, which is harvested every fifteen to eighteen days from May to October.

but despite the odds, the world's most northern tea gardens are being developed in Oregon's Willamette Valley and Washington's Skagit Valley. The long-term goal of the tea-growing team of Rob Miller and John Vendeland is to bring these experimental gardens to full-scale commercial production, but that dream will take time to realize.

Right now, the only full-scale tea production occurring in the United States is in South Carolina, one of the states that took part in the country's initial tea-growing attempts in the late 1800s. Tea plants at the Charleston Tea Gardens (formerly called Charleston Tea Plantation) are descendants of these plants, growing on an old Lipton Tea experimental plantation on Wadmalaw Island, near Charleston, South Carolina. The 127-acre plantation is home to American Classic Tea—the dream project of Englishman William Barclay Hall, a third-generation professional tea taster, and tea horticulturist Mack Fleming, a former long-time employee of the Thomas J. Lipton Company.

In 2003 Bigelow Tea purchased the Charleston Tea Plantation and renamed it the Charleston Tea Gardens. Hall remained on staff to oversee the operation. The Charleston Tea Gardens continues to produce tea with the American Classic Tea label. Public tours of the gardens are available.

ORGANIC, BIODYNAMIC, AND FAIR TRADE ALTERNATIVES

As consumers seek to buy earth-friendly products, producers eventually step up to meet the demand. A good example is products made from recyclable materials. Once rare, now recycling and recycled materials touch every area of our lives, from the packaging of the food we buy, to the clothes we wear and the homes we live in, to even how we discard our garbage. Organic products may be the next wave of popular environmental consumerism, and tea is clearly part of the picture. Sage Group International, producer of the *Tea Is "Hot" Report*, predicts the certified-organic tea market will reach the area of $125 million in sales, up from just $7.6 million in 2000.

Organic Tea

India, Sri Lanka, and China are leaders in organic tea production.

Tea labeled "organic" does not ensure quality, but it does certify the tea is grown without using any chemical fertilizers, pesticides, or herbicides for at least three years. Instead, tea growers use natural methods to fertilize and control pests and disease, while protecting the health of humans and the environment. An independent certifying agency verifies tea growers comply with stringent, internationally recognized organic guidelines. India, Sri Lanka, and China are leaders in organic tea production.

It may be helpful to distinguish between "all-natural" and "organic" food products. All-natural means it was made without artificial or synthetic ingredients, but it does not address how the ingredients were grown. Chemical fertilizers and pesticides may have been used. Organic refers to specific methods for growing and processing food.

Biodynamic Tea Plantations

Biodynamic agriculture takes the basic principles of organic farming to the next dimension. It is a holistic approach to the process, transforming a tea plantation

Organic Standards

In the United States, there is an alphabet soup of organizations governing the standards of organic products. The OFPA (Organic Food Protection Act) requires the USDA (U.S. Department of Agriculture) to develop national organic standards using guidelines of the OFPA and the NOP (National Organic Program) that stipulate the products must come from sources accredited by the USDA. It sounds complicated, but it's very simple for the tea drinker. Tea displaying the "USDA Organic" seal means it has been certified to contain at least 95 percent organically produced ingredients.

into a self-contained ecosystem. Farming activities on the plantation are aligned with our solar system's natural forces, such as following the rhythm of the lunar calendar and super-charging compost heaps with herbal applications. The emphasis is on the well-being of the plantation workers and their harmonious relationship with nature and the environment. Successful examples of biodynamic tea plantations can be found in India and Sri Lanka.

Fair Trade Tea

Fair trade certified tea means the tea is grown on an estate that provides its workers with fair wages, safe working conditions, adequate housing, and healthcare and education for their families. In addition to the price of the tea, licensed tea importers pay a fair trade premium that goes into a tea plantation's community development fund. These funds are democratically managed by estate managers and the workers. Currently there are fair trade certified tea estates in India, Nepal, Sri Lanka, Vietnam, China, Tanzania, Kenya, Zimbabwe, and Uganda that benefit 120,000 tea pickers and their families.

Tea is the most consumed beverage next to water and also the most affordable. The cost for a cup of tea is nearly as varied as the variety of teas available, from about 4 cents per tea bag for an inexpensive grocery store brand to over $200 for a pound of rare, loose leaf tea. Two hundred dollars a pound may not sound like a good value until it's put in perspective. A pound of poultry might be $5, top sirloin about $6 to $7, but how many servings will you get for your money? A pound of tea will make about 200 cups of tea. So a serving of the most rare, costly tea would be less expensive than a bottle of name-brand soda pop. You can also buy loose leaf tea in very small quantities of one to two ounces. At my local tea shop, the Carnelian Rose Tea Co., many wonderful teas are priced at $6.95 for a quarter pound, which is less than 14 cents a cup. So why wouldn't you treat yourself to the best tea money can buy? Maybe a handpicked oolong from the misty mountaintop of China's Wuyi Mountains or a first flush Darjeeling from a terraced slope on a Himalayan hilltop? Not only is tea a terrific value, but its long-lasting health effects may be priceless. In the next chapter, we'll take a look at some of the claims concerning the health benefits of tea, prompting the question: myth or science? You may be surprised at the results.

CHAPTER 5

ToYourHealth!

*My experience . . . convinced me that tea was better than brandy,
and during the last six months in Africa I took no brandy,
even when sick, taking tea instead.*

—THEODORE ROOSEVELT, 1912 LETTER

President Theodore Roosevelt believed what many scientists are proving today. Tea is good for you. This is a revelation that has come full circle. In its earliest use, tea was touted for its medicinal properties. In the *Pen Ts'ao*, a medical book dating back to ancient China, tea is noted for its invigorating effect on the body, good for a variety of aliments from head to toe. In the eighth century book, *The Classic of Tea*, author Lu Yu suggests drinking four or five cups of tea if one is "given to melancholia, suffering from aching of the brain, smarting of the eyes, troubled in the four limbs or afflicted in the hundred joints." English coffeehouse owner Thomas Garway introduced tea to the Western world in 1658.

In the first advertisement for the new drink, he informed his audience it had been endorsed by the entire medical profession, saying, "That excellent, and by all physitians approved China drink."

Even today, people who do not regularly drink tea often instinctively turn to tea when they're sick. Many recall childhood remedies of hot tea with honey to relieve sore throats and flu. But what modern science is studying today goes far beyond soothing common cold and flu symptoms. Tea may possess impressive curative properties for strokes, heart disease, and many kinds of cancer. Some studies show tea can promote bone health, aid weight loss, alleviate arthritis, and even help stop bad breath and tooth decay.

WHAT'S IN THE LEAF?

Before looking at recent studies on the health benefits of "true" tea (*Camellia sinensis*), let's consider the properties of the leaf. Tea leaves contain vitamins, minerals, caffeine, and polyphenols. While caffeine may play an important role in the overall health benefits of tea, most studies have focused on its main component, polyphenols. Polyphenols are naturally occurring compounds found in most plants. Their presence in fruits, vegetables, and especially red wine and tea has garnered plenty of recent media attention for their powerful vitamin-like antioxidant capabilities to attack potentially harmful free radicals in the body.

Free radicals are unstable molecules, by-products of the body's normal chemical processes, which can damage DNA and cell membranes. Imagine your body as a healthy home, and the free radicals are the debris that collects in the wastebaskets. If you have stress in your house, some alcohol consumption, maybe a smoker or two, even more debris collects. If it's not removed, the debris can become a source of disease. The cell damage caused by these free radicals in the body can lead to aging and illnesses like cancer, heart attacks, and stroke. Polyphenols can neutralize the harmful effects of these free radicals and may help prevent blood clotting. Acting as scavengers, or in this example, house cleaners, the polyphenols bind with the free radicals and cancel out their damaging effects.

Tea has the blessing of all deities, promotes filial piety, drives away the devil, banishes drowsiness, keeps the five viscera in harmony, wards off disease, strengthens friendships disciplines body and mind, destroys the passions, gives peaceful death.

—Myoe Shonin (1173–1232), Japanese Buddhist Priest

Flavonoids

Tea leaves are rich in flavonoids, a category of polyphenols. An important factor in the flavonoid content of a tea leaf is how the leaf is processed (white, green, oolong, or black). Catechins are a class of simple flavonoids found in high concentrations in green and white tea and lower concentrations in black and oolong tea. The oxidation of black and oolong tea changes the catechins to more complex flavonoids, called theaflavins and thearubigins, not found in green tea. According to the Tea Council of the United States, research discussed at the Third International Scientific Symposium on Tea and Human Health in 2002 shows simple flavonoids are quickly absorbed in the body, but complex flavonoids are metabolized in other areas, leading scientists to consider the greater health advantages. In fact, Jeffrey B. Blumberg, PhD, co-chair of the Symposium, states the following:

> Because green and black tea flavonoids appear to be absorbed and metabolized at different points throughout the digestion process, flavonoids may have an even wider range of protective benefits to various body systems than originally thought.

EGCG in Tea

Epigallocatechin-3-gallate (EGCG) is an especially powerful catechin in tea. The subject of numerous scientific studies, it packs an antioxidant punch many times stronger than vitamins C and E. In fact, researchers from the Medical College of Ohio in Toledo discovered EGCG may halt cancer growth. They found EGCG suppressed the activity of urokinase, a protein that gives cancer cells their ability to grow and spread in the body. In later research at the college, scientists found EGCG killed 100 percent of bladder cancer cells in a test tube study; and when injected into cancerous bladder tumors in laboratory mice, the EGCG blocked cancer growth in 64 percent of the mice.

Dr. Blumberg is the Associate Director and Chief of Antioxidants Research Laboratory and Senior Scientist at the USDA Jean Mayer Human Nutrition Research Center on Aging, located at Tufts University.

Laboratory studies found that EGCG, a particularly powerful catechin in tea (see "EGCG in Tea" on page 91), enhanced the effectiveness of the breast cancer drug tamoxifen. When researchers at Saitama Prefectural Cancer Center in Japan combined EGCG in a test tube with tamoxifen and breast cancer cells, it resulted in the death of twice as many cancer cells compared to the results of tamoxifen alone. In another Japanese study of 472 stage I and II breast cancer patients, researchers found a possible link between green tea consumption and the rate of breast cancer recurrence after seven years. Patients drinking five or more cups of green tea a day had a recurrence rate of 16.7 percent, compared to 24.3 percent recurrence for patients drinking four cups or less per day. And a recent study at the University of Southern California in Los Angeles found that Asian-American women who drank green tea had a significantly reduced risk of breast cancer.

Polyphenols in green and black tea reduced the level of a prostrate cancer protein shown to protect cancer cells from dying. Researchers from the H. Lee Moffitt Cancer Center in Tampa, Florida, found the higher the concentration of polyphenols, the more cancer cells died. And Researchers at the University of Wisconsin's Department of Dermatology found prostrate cancer growth was markedly suppressed when mice, genetically predisposed to the disease, were given the daily equivalent of about six cups of green tea.

With much of the scientific focus on the high concentrations of EGCG in green tea, many may wonder how black tea stacks up. Because it is most popular in the West, more scientific studies are focusing on black tea and discovering its health benefits are comparable to green tea. In fact, researchers have identified a polyphenol compound in black tea that can stop cancer. It's called theaflavin-3'-monogallate, or TF-2. Laboratory tests at Rutgers University in New Jersey showed TF-2 caused colorectal cancer cells to die while healthy cells thrived. In addition, TF-2 was found to suppress a gene associated with colon cancer.

Cream or sugar? Science has also found that adding milk to tea does not stop

The Comeback Tea

Recent reports claiming green tea may help prevent cardiovascular disease, bone loss, certain cancers, and even fight cavities and aid weight loss, are fueling its comeback. It may seem as though green tea is too new to the Western market to stage a return, yet 40 percent of the tea consumed prior to World War II was green. During the war, tea trade with the East was suspended, so the West satisfied its demand with more black tea, especially from India. Although green tea is still the preferred tea in the East, black tea is the tea of choice in the rest of the world, accounting for approximately 78 percent of the tea produced and consumed worldwide. Green tea accounts for about 22 percent, and oolong less than 2 percent. Despite these statistics, green tea consumption has made some significant leaps in the last few years.

In the late 1990s, less than 5 percent of the tea consumed in the US every year was green tea, but by 2002, its use more than doubled, jumping between 8 and 9 percent. In the early- to mid-1990s, news stories on the health benefits of tea told consumers to look for green tea in health food stores and Asian markets. Now, it's so popular, tea companies produce many varieties of scented and blended green teas, commonly found on grocery store shelves next to long-time favorite black tea blends. Companies are also capitalizing on green tea's healthful reputation by using it in hair and skin products, dietary supplements, gum, candy, even aromatherapy products. According to the highly respected Tea Is "Hot" Report, green tea is predicted to outsell black tea in the United States by the year 2008.

the body from absorbing tea's antioxidants. In fact, adding milk to tea provides additional health benefits, especially when fortified with vitamins and minerals. Other studies have shown that adding sugar, sweetener, or lemon to tea does not diminish its antioxidant effects. And tea is not significantly inhibited by decaffeination. Also iced tea, because it's brewed first, is just as healthy as hot tea if prepared with equal amounts of leaves and water. If you dilute your iced tea with added water, consider adding more leaves to the infusion.

Of course, the amount of sugar added to tea, hot or cold, is an important

Tea is an inexpensive,
delicious drink that
contains no fats,
calories, or sugar.
What could be
better than that?

consideration for your health. Some ready-to-drink bottled iced teas can contain as many as fifteen teaspoons of sugar. Tea is an inexpensive and delicious drink that, in its purest form, contains no fat, calories, or sugar. What could be better?

Throughout the world, a countless number of research studies have been—and continue to be—conducted on the health benefits of tea. Some studies focus on either black or green tea, others study oolong, and a few consider white tea. Some researchers include several types of teas in their studies. The following information on a variety of health issues reflects the results of many of these studies.

CANCER

In 2003, the American Cancer Society estimated that 1.33 million cases of cancer were diagnosed in the United States, and approximately 556,500 died of the disease. It's a frightening fact. And while science races to find a cure, some people are satisfied to sit, quietly sipping their tea. Laboratory mice have been doing just that for decades. In an article titled "Tea Complements Drugs In Fight Against Colon Cancer," Gayle A. Orner, PhD, of Oregon State University's Linus Pauling Institute, explains that:

> Teas exert significant protective effects in experimental animal models of skin, lung, esophageal, gastric, hepatic, small intestinal, pancreatic, colon, bladder and mammary cancer

Colon and Rectal Cancer

Colon and rectal cancer are the third leading cause of cancer deaths in the United States for both men and women. The Linus Pauling Institute at Oregon State University (OSU) has been studying the effects of both green and white tea on colon cancer. Green tea is recognized for its high concentration of EGCG, but white tea is just beginning to be studied. The least processed of tea types, white tea has the most preserved catechins. In the OSU study, white tea brewed under the same conditions as green tea showed some higher concentrations of antioxidants, indicating that white tea may provide greater health benefits than black, oolong, or green tea.

In the OSU study, two groups of laboratory mice were given water or white tea for eight weeks, while also receiving a carcinogen similar to those that can form on the surface of grilled, broiled, or fried meats. These substances can set off cell changes that may develop into cancer. Scientists found a significantly lower incidence of pre-cancerous colon tumors in mice that drank white tea than in the group that drank only water.

In another study, researchers at the Linus Pauling Institute used laboratory mice, genetically predisposed to develop tumors, to compare the cancer-fighting effectiveness of white tea, green tea, and a commonly used colon cancer drug called sulindac. Mice given green tea had a reduced number of colon polyps, from an average of 30 to 17; but those given white tea dropped the average number of polyps from 30 to 13. White tea and sulindac combined reduced the average number of polyps about 80 percent, from 30 to 6, indicating that combining the tea with traditional cancer treatment could prove more effective. Previous research showed sulindac alone reduced polyp development by about half. However, treatment with sulindac and other non-steroidal anti-inflammatory drugs can produce side effects, while treatment with tea did not.

Tobacco and DNA Damage

Researchers at the University of Rochester's Environmental Health Science Center in New York found EGCG and EGC (epigallocathechin) in green tea can help stop cancer growth by blocking the activity of a molecule manipulated by dioxins and tobacco smoke. And a nine-year study of 8,552 Japanese adults found that drinking ten or more cups of green tea a day delayed the onset of cancer 8.7 years in women and 3 years in men, when compared to study participants who drank less than three cups of tea per day.

As science begins to investigate the preventative power of white tea, the media takes note and suddenly interest in tea shops increases. Before long, white tea will be as readily available on supermarket shelves as black or green tea. But for now, unless you just want to enjoy its delicate flavor, it is unnecessary to seek out white tea to benefit from tea's powerful antioxidants.

It seems more and more that drinking tea is something like drinking a vegetable, and it sure beats drinking brewed spinach leaves.

—John H. Weisburger, PhD, MD (hon.) American Health Foundation, *Prevention*, May 1996

The connection between tea drinking and healthier smokers seemed to be linked in a clinical study discussed at the Third International Scientific Symposium on Tea and Human Health. The study reported smokers who drank four cups of decaffeinated green or black tea a day showed blood and urine levels with a marked reduction in oxidative stress, or DNA damage, believed to be a cause in developing many chronic diseases including cancer. In addition, a study of 855 male smokers in Uruguay found those who drank two or more cups of black tea a day had a 66-percent reduced risk of lung cancer.

Skin Cancer

America is a sun-loving nation, and medical science can prove it with skin cancer rates climbing faster than you can say, "please pass the suntan oil." Skin cancer is the most common form of cancer in the United States, affecting approximately one million people a year. It can take years of chasing the sun for deep tan lines, but eventually the sun exposure some crave to acquire "healthy" looking skin turns deadly for nearly 10,000 Americans every year. And while sipping iced tea might sound like a good way to cool down on a hot summer afternoon, using tea for protection from potentially harmful ultraviolet rays is a completely new idea. But research is proving tea may be as good a sunscreen as a thirst-quencher.

Scientists are demonstrating amazing success studying tea's preventative properties against skin cancer. At Rutgers University, laboratory mice were separated into four groups, each drinking only one of four kinds of tea for thirty-one weeks: green or black, both regular and decaffeinated. A control group drank only water. During the study the mice were exposed to two carcinogens known to cause cancer. The tea-drinking mice developed 70 percent to 90 percent fewer skin cancers than the control group. Green and black tea were equally effective, and the decaffeinated teas showed only slightly reduced results.

In another Rutgers University study, researchers exposed laboratory mice to ultraviolet light two times a week for five months, accelerating their chances for developing skin cancer. They were then divided into three groups, and five days a week over the next eighteen weeks, researchers applied a medicated lotion of either caffeine or EGCG to the mice. The control group's lotion was inactive. Compared to the control group, the mice rubbed with the caffeinated lotion developed 44 percent fewer non-cancerous tumors and 72 percent fewer cancerous tumors. The mice rubbed with the EGCG lotion showed a 55-percent reduction in non-cancerous tumors and 65 percent fewer cancerous tumors.

The results of the Rutgers University studies were echoed by scientists at Ohio's Case Western Reserve University (CWRU). Researchers at the university's Skin Diseases Research Center exposed laboratory mice to ultraviolet light after either feeding them green tea or applying EGCG to their skin. Mice given either form of the tea polyphenols developed fewer cancerous tumors, and the topical application was also found to help prevent non-cancerous lesions from becoming cancerous.

When they stepped up the research to human trials, scientists at CWRU used

Keep Those Used Tea Bags!

A cup of tea is often credited as possessing soothing properties, but have you ever considered using tea as a method to soothe your skin? The secret is the tannin compounds in the tea bag, an astringent substance with antibacterial and antiviral powers that are found only in "real tea," not herbal tea. After you've steeped your brew and drunk the tea, don't discard the bag. There are claims that a cooled tea bag offers relief from a number of conditions when placed directly on the troubled area. The touch of the tea bag is said to:

- cleanse and numb canker sores
- reduce the swelling of puffy eyes
- stop the bleeding from tooth extractions
- help heal eye infections
- soothe sunburned skin

Just make sure the tea bag has cooled off a bit!

light-skinned volunteers to put green tea to the test. After applying green tea polyphenols to the backsides of six volunteers, researchers exposed them to ultraviolet light. Test results found green tea polyphenols helped protect the volunteers' skin from DNA damage, which can cause skin cancer.

Other Cancers

Studies in Shanghai, China, have shown a link between drinking green tea and the prevention of lung, esophageal, and stomach cancers. Researchers from the National Cancer Institute and the Shanghai Cancer Institute studied 902 esophageal cancer patients aged 30 to 74 over a twenty-eight-month period, comparing them to a control group of 1,552 people. Green tea drinkers who did not smoke or drink alcohol had a 60-percent lower risk of esophageal cancer than non-tea drinkers.

Research indicates that lung cancer risks decrease with increased tea drinking.

A two-year study of 1,324 Shanghai women, 649 with lung cancer, found that non-smokers who drank green tea had a reduced risk of lung cancer. The study also found that lung cancer risks of non-smokers decreased with increased consumption of tea.

Additionally, a twenty-seven-month Shanghai study of 711 stomach cancer patients and an equal number in a control group, found people who drank at least one cup of green tea a week for six months or longer showed a 30-percent lower risk of stomach cancer, compared to non-tea drinkers.

Science has also found green tea polyphenols can reduce the risk of chronic gastritis as much as 50 percent. Chronic gastritis is an inflammatory disease causing stomach lesions that can lead to cancer. The study, from the School of Public Health and Jonsson Comprehensive Cancer Center at UCLA, also reported that using green tea to treat the disease would decrease the long-term occurrence of stomach cancer. And an eight-year Iowa Women's Health Study found of the 35,369 post-menopausal women participants, those who drank two or more cups of (primarily black) tea per day had a significantly lower risk of developing urinary and digestive tract cancer, compared to non-tea drinking women.

Tea for All Ages

Some may think enjoying a calm cuppa is synonymous with maturity; that people who'd prefer to spend the evening with Earl Grey rather than Jack Daniels, wear comfortable shoes and button their shirt collars. Well, they haven't met the members of The Tea Association (TTA), a group of young Norwegian men who have come together for their love of tea. A quick peek at their website shows eleven bare-chested young men posing for the camera— no shirt collars to button on this group of teetotalers. They have a dream, "A world full of tea and happiness—a world without pain." While the young Nordic men extol the virtues of a tea-filled existence, they do adhere to a few rules, or commandments, as they call them.

The Tea Association's Five Commandments:

1. Thou shall have no other hot drink than Tea!

2. Thou shalt not abuse the name of Tea.

3. Thou shall hold the day of Teas, Thursday, sacred.

4. Thou shalt not drink coffee.

5. Thou shalt not lust for thy friend's Tea.

And finally, a Russian study further linked the cancer-fighting benefits of tea drinking for women, finding black tea may reduce the incidence of rectal cancer. Women participants who consumed high levels of tea were shown to have a 60-percent reduction in the risk of rectal cancer, while moderate tea drinking showed a 52-percent risk reduction, as compared to women in the low-consumption group. The research, discussed at the Third International Scientific Symposium on Tea and Human Health, defined high consumption as more than 160 grams dry tea per month (equivalent to approximately eighty cups of tea); moderate consumption as 80 to 160 grams per month; and low tea consumption was less than 80 grams per month.

What is the future of tea and cancer research? Prevention, rather than cure, is becoming increasingly important. Cancer studies are underway at the University of South Carolina where two researchers, Dr. Michael Wargovich and Dr. Theresa

"Mr. Churchill, if I were your wife, I'd put poison in your tea."

"Madam, were I your husband, I would surely drink it."

—An exchange between Lady Astor and Winston Churchill

Smith, funded by a $1.2 million grant from the National Institutes of Health, are investigating whether drinking tea will help prevent colon cancer. The study will seek to identify the active components that give green and black tea cancer-preventing properties. We can expect many future studies demonstrating the remarkable preventative and therapeutic effects of tea on cancer.

HEART DISEASE AND STROKES

According to the American Heart Association, 42 million Americans have high cholesterol, a significant risk factor for heart disease. A number of studies have shown the antioxidant power of tea flavonoids can prevent low-density lipoproteins (LDLs), or bad cholesterol, from binding with free radicals in the body and undergoing a process called oxidation. Lower LDL levels reduce the risk of atherosclerosis, a narrowing of the artery wall caused by fatty plaque buildup due to oxidized LDL, which can lead to heart disease and strokes.

According to research published in the November 1995 *Journal of Agriculture and Food Chemistry*, tea flavonoids prevented LDL cholesterol from clogging blood vessels in a laboratory study. Scientists discovered that of the over thirty antioxidants investigated, tea's high concentration of EGCG was the most powerful. And in the first tea study to strictly control participants' diet, researchers at Maryland's USDA Beltsville Human Nutrition Research Center found drinking five cups of tea a day could lower LDL cholesterol by 10 percent when combined with a diet moderately low in fat and cholesterol.

Heart Attacks

Heart disease is America's number-one killer and a heart attack is the most recognized evidence of the disease. In 1999, two studies were released that show daily tea drinking could significantly reduce the risk of heart attack. Over a one-year period, 340 heart attack sufferers were studied at Boston's Brigham and Women's Hospital and Harvard Medical School. Participants were examined for their coffee and tea drinking habits, and compared to people with similar characteristics including location, age, and sex, but who had not suffered a heart attack. The results showed people drinking one or more cups of tea a day cut their risk of heart attack by 44 percent, but showed no link between drinking coffee and reduced incidence of heart attacks.

In the fall of 1999, results of a larger study showed even more dramatic findings. An investigation in the Netherlands of 3,454 people, aged 55 or older, revealed that those who drank one to two cups of black tea a day reduced their risk of heart disease by 46 percent. People who drank four or more cups of tea cut their risk by 69 percent. And a recent study in Saudi Arabia of 3,430 men and women aged 30 to 70, found those drinking more than six cups of black tea a day had more than a 50-percent lower risk of developing heart disease compared to non-tea drinkers.

For those who have suffered a heart attack, tea drinking could prolong their life. A Harvard Medical School study interviewed 1,900 patients an average of four days after their heart attack. Those who drank fourteen or more cups of tea a week had a 44-percent lower death rate during the follow-up period (which averaged 3.8 years), compared to non-tea drinking patients. Study patients who drank less than fourteen cups of tea a week had a 28-percent lower death rate.

People who drink tea regularly may have a reduced risk of heart disease.

Strokes

According to the American Stroke Association, about 700,000 Americans suffered a stroke in 2003, or one every 45 seconds. About 83 percent of strokes are caused by an obstruction, typically a blood clot. An Australian study showed tea drinking may help prevent blood clots from forming. In an eight-week trial of 22 participants, researchers divided the study into two parts. During the first four weeks, all participants drank five cups of hot water a day. In the last four weeks, all drank five cups of black tea each day. The study, conducted at the University of Western Australia Department of Medicine and HeartSearch, Royal

Perth Hospital, showed the tea drinkers had considerably reduced blood levels of P-selectin, a substance associated with blood coagulation.

In addition, a fifteen-year investigation in the Netherlands showed that tea drinking may reduce the incidence of stroke. Researchers studied 552 men between the ages of 50 and 69, and found those who consumed 4.7 cups of black tea daily were 69 percent less likely to suffer a stroke than the men who drank less than 2.6 cups of tea a day. And in a four-year study of 5,910 Japanese women who did not smoke or drink alcohol, researchers found that the occurrence of stroke was significantly lower in women who drank at least three to four cups of green tea a day.

ORAL HEALTH

The garlic-roasted chicken was wonderful, but now you'll have to keep everyone at arm's length until you can brush your teeth. A stick of gum or breath mint may be a temporary fix, but a cup of tea would be more effective, especially if you swish before you swallow. Bad breath, or halitosis, is caused by volatile sulfur compounds (VSC) produced by bacteria in our mouths. Studies have shown that polyphenols in tea can stop the growth of bacteria that cause bad breath, and also inhibit growth and acid production of plaque bacteria that cause cavities and gum disease.

Researchers at the University of British Columbia studied a variety of treatments for bad breath, including gum and mints, and found that green tea was more effective at killing VSC. Researchers at the University of Illinois at Chicago (UIC) College of Dentistry found black tea polyphenols reduced the production of a bacterial enzyme associated with bad breath by 30 percent. Earlier studies at the UIC College of Dentistry found black tea reduces dental plaque by blocking bacteria that help plaque stick to teeth.

In a collaborative study, researchers at the Institute of Odontology at Sweden's Göteborg University studied ten volunteers who rinsed their mouths with black tea for one minute, ten times a day, compared to a control group who rinsed with only water. Results showed those who rinsed with tea had less plaque buildup and acid on their teeth, and plaque with less cavity-causing bacteria.

The tea plant also contains fluoride, which it draws from the soil and collects in its leaves. Many factors effect tea's fluoride content. Green tea, for example, has a much higher fluoride content than black tea. According to several studies, the Tea Council of the United Kingdom reported that brewed tea contains between 0.34 and 6 parts per million of fluoride. Based on standards set by the United States Public Health Service, fluoridated water in the United States contains a concentration of fluoride between 0.7 and 1.2 parts per million. Recognized for its cavity-fighting abilities, fluoride strengthens tooth enamel, increasing its resistance to decay. A recent study showed that 34 percent of the fluoride remained in the mouths of study participants who rinsed with tea. Other studies conducted on laboratory animals showed tea reduced cavity activity by 50 to 75 percent. Researchers at Forsyth Dental Center in Boston found that tea exceeded the cavity-fighting abilities of any other foods tested.

In addition to halitosis and tooth decay, tea may prevent mouth cancer. Research at the Chinese Academy of Preventive Medicine studied 59 patients with precancerous mouth lesions. Over a six-month period, green and black tea extracts were applied on the lesions of 29 patients, while a placebo was applied to the lesions in the control group. The result was a reduction of lesion size in 37.9 percent of the treated group and only a 10-percent reduction in the control group.

BONE HEALTH

"Got tea?" is a phrase that could become popular, due to recent research in England and Taiwan linking tea to stronger bones. The National Osteoporosis Foundation reports that osteoporosis, or porous bone, is a health threat for 44 million Americans: 10 million estimated to have the disease, and 34 million who have low bone mass, putting them at risk. In the studies scientists speculated tea's flavonoids, fluoride, and phytoestrogens, with their estrogen-like effect, may all help to preserve bone density and protect against osteoporosis.

Addressing concerns that too much fluoride can be toxic, noted physician and author, Dr. Andrew Weil, reported on his website (www.drweil.com), "Fluoride is toxic in very large quantities and can cause gastrointestinal symptoms and sometimes even death. But you'd have to ingest about 20,000 times more fluoride than what's in an 8-ounce glass of fluoridated water to see such an effect."

In a bone mineral density (BMD) study of 1,256 English women, aged from 65 to 76, researchers found the 1,134 women who drank at least one cup of tea a day had five percent more BMD in the base of their spine and two hip regions than non-tea drinkers, which could mean a 10- to 15-percent reduction in fracture risk. The study, conducted by the University of Cambridge School of Medicine and Addenbrooke's Hospital, also noted that these results were independent of the number of cups of tea consumed, whether or not the women smoked, drank coffee, used milk, or hormone replacement therapy.

A woman is like a tea bag. It's only when she is in hot water that you realize how strong she is.

—Anonymous

In a study researchers claim is the first of its kind, scientists investigated green, black, and oolong tea drinking in both sexes. In a survey of 497 men and 540 women, aged 30 and older, researchers at the National Cheng Kung University Hospital in Taiwan found that habitual drinking of any tea type over a long period of time appears to strengthen bones in both men and women. Habitual tea drinkers were defined as those who routinely drank tea for at least one year. Study participants who routinely drank tea for ten or more years had hip bone density 6.2 percent higher than participants who were non-habitual tea drinkers. Participants who routinely drank tea for six to ten years had 2.3 percent higher hip bone density compared to the non-habitual tea drinkers. Researchers also noted the body's total BMD was improved in the habitual tea drinkers, and that it was the duration, rather than the amount of the tea drinking, that resulted in the increased bone density.

WEIGHT LOSS

We've covered some remarkable research findings concerning the health benefits of tea and its effect on cancer, heart disease, stroke, tooth decay, and bone health. The results are so compelling you might be thinking, "I should drink more tea." Well, the latest research may further inspire you to do just that, because science has found green tea appears to help burn calories faster.

Researchers at the University of Geneva in Switzerland studied ten healthy young men of varying weights for six weeks. The men maintained the same diet

Tea Tips the Political Scales!

A beautiful young woman, a powerful political figure, and an impeached president. A familiar story? Maybe not. The President is Andrew Johnson, the young woman is artist Vinnie Ream, and the politician is Republican Senator Edmund Ross of Kansas.

The year is 1868. Democratic President Andrew Johnson has just been impeached for high crimes and misdemeanors stemming from his opposition to post-Civil War congressional reconstruction. The President is on trial in the Senate, and the Republicans want him out. But Senator Ross has the deciding vote and he has not announced which way he'll cast it. Tensions are high and tea is about to be served.

Enter Miss Ream, a petite and pretty 18-year-old sculptor from Kansas. A longtime family friend of Senator Ross, Miss Ream became a boarder in his Washington, DC home. She had won a $10,000 federal commission to sculpt a marble statue of slain President Abraham Lincoln. This was shocking to many, since Miss Ream was the first woman, and youngest person, ever to receive such an honor. But because she was attractive and had close ties with the Senator, she fell victim to suspicion and accusations as to the real reason for her good fortune.

It was said Miss Ream had considerable charm and influence with men. It's believed she supported President Johnson, and that Senator Ross's refusal to declare his position was due to her influence. The night before the vote, Senator Ross remained at home and refused to talk to anyone. The Republicans wanted to know how he would vote, so they sent a Johnson opponent and reputed ladies man to the Senator's home to charm his way past Miss Ream. He was no match for the strong-willed artist, who fended off his attempts to talk to the Senator with cups of tea. After hours of exertion—and endless cups of tea—the young man got his answer, but not from the Senator. Miss Ream declared the Senator would vote not guilty—and he did.

and exercise, the only difference was every day with their meals they were given either green tea extract with 50 milligrams of caffeine, 50 milligrams of caffeine alone, or a placebo. The participants taking the green tea extract (equivalent to about four cups of tea) used more calories and burned more fat each day than the men who took only caffeine or the placebo. Scientists speculate EGCG in green tea stimulates the body to burn calories, increasing metabolism by about 4 percent. Even more good news is the heart rate of the men taking the green tea extract did not increase, indicating green tea may be a substitute for caffeine-based diet pills. In fact, diet pills made with green tea extract are common today.

AND THERE'S MORE

If all that research isn't enough to convince you drinking tea is good for you, a recent study revealed drinking tea every day may boost your body's natural immunity to fight bacterial infections, thanks to a chemical called L-theanine found in tea. And in a five-month study at the Department of Microbiology and Immunology at Showa University School of Medicine in Japan, test results showed participants who gargled twice a day with a mouthwash containing black tea extract had a higher immunity to influenza infection.

Green tea may also offer relief for arthritis sufferers. Studies at Ohio's Case Western Reserve University found green tea polyphenols may have anti-inflammatory properties that can help prevent rheumatoid arthritis and decrease the intensity of its symptoms. Researchers found 56 percent of mice given the equiv-

The Color of Tea

Tea as a beverage has many benefits, but you don't need to drink tea to appreciate its unique qualities.

Use strong black tea as a coloring agent. Are you bored with the color of your couch cover or the shade of your shirt? Is that once-crisp white blouse hopelessly discolored? If so, soak the fabric in tea. During World War II, nylons were costly and in short supply, so ladies dyed their rag tag collection of nylons in tea to give them uniform color.

You can also use tea to make the young look old and the old look young. Soak fabric in tea to give fabric dolls and housewares, like table linens, an antique look. Even a wet tea bag applied to paper will give an aged look to an invitation or special gift. And instead of buying expensive hair dye, try rinsing gray hair in a rinse of strong black tea.

alent of four cups of green tea a day did not develop collagen-induced arthritis, and of the 44 percent that did, their symptoms were less severe; while 94 percent of the mice given only water developed the disease.

And finally, tea may even help prevent Parkinson's disease and enhance insulin activity. The Department of Environmental Health at the University of Washington's School of Public Health and Community Medicine conducted a study on Parkinson's disease and found that drinking two or more cups of tea per day may reduce the risk of developing the disease. Meanwhile, in an initial study of volunteers with type II diabetes, scientists at the Lipid Metabolism Laboratory, at the USDA Jean Mayer Human Nutrition Research Center on Aging, located at Tufts University, found a high flavonoid diet that included drinking six cups of black tea a day lowered blood sugar levels by 15 to 20 percent.

Tea may even provide some allergy relief. Laboratory tests at Kyushu University in Fukuoka, Japan, found that EGCG blocked the body's production of compounds involved in setting off and sustaining allergic reactions.

While scientific research is exploring the amazing potential of tea to prevent and protect against many diseases, scientists would be the first to say that tea is not a substitute for a healthy diet. The test results are inconclusive and much more research must be done. So while they sort out the test results and ponder the health benefits, we can continue to enjoy the simple pleasures of a cup of tea, knowing it may also be very good for us. But just how much tea should we drink to reap the potential health benefits? As we've seen, a Japanese study suggests ten or more cups, while an Australian study determined five; a Dutch study suggests four or more; an Iowa study suggests at least two; researchers in England found positive results with as little as one cup of tea per day; and a Taiwan study found the best results came from long-term tea drinking, rather than the amount of tea consumed. Clearly, science has not determined an exact number.

What we do know, however, is that tea does not contain any fats, additives, artificial colors or flavorings, so we are limited in our enjoyment of this ancient elixir only by the amount of caffeine in the cup. And if caffeine is a concern, brew decaffeinated tea instead. Another way to enjoy tea is to cook with it. In the next two chapters, we'll explore recipes for hot and cold beverages, tea treats, and even side dishes and main meals—all made with "real" and herbal teas.

Part Two

The **Tastes** & **Pleasures** of the **Tea Leaf**

BEVERAGES & RECIPES

The next two chapters in *Tales of a Tea Leaf* contain a collection of recipes all made with "real" or herbal teas—hot and cold drinks, breads, cakes, pies, side dishes, soup, sauces, and even main meals. They were created by individuals and in company kitchens, and the wide variety of tastes represented is a testament to the many exciting ways tea can be incorporated into your kitchen, not just your teapot.

Because the sources vary, so do the methods of preparation. Some call for tea bags, others loose leaf tea, and a few are herbal creations. With the permission to use these recipes comes the responsibility to keep them in their original form. Some simple guidelines will help you as you experiment with the recipes.

When the recipe calls for a tea bag and you would prefer to use loose leaf tea, or vice versa, substitute one teaspoon of tea for a tea bag. Always use fresh, cold water when preparing tea. If the recipe calls for strong tea, just double the amount of tea you would normally use. For example, if the recipe calls for two cups of strong black tea, use four tea bags or four teaspoons of tea.

Many recipes do not specify a particular variety of tea. In this case, use your favorite tea, or try something new. If an iced tea recipe calls for only a black tea, try one that is fruit-flavored. Experimenting is half the fun!

CHAPTER 6

CoolCreationsand HotandHealingBrews

Meanwhile, let us have a sip of tea.
The afternoon glow is brightening the bamboos,
the fountains are bubbling with delight,
the soughing of the pines is heard in our kettle.
Let us dream of evanescence, and linger
in the beautiful foolishness of things.

—KAKUZO OKAKURA, *THE BOOK OF TEA*

Tea is the quintessential comfort drink. Hot tea warms us when we're cold and iced tea cools us when we're hot. We share a pot or pitcher of tea to welcome friends, or enjoy a solitary cup to cheer us when we're alone. It wakes us in the morning and calms us in the evening. Tea is truly a universal elixir of limitless charm and purpose. Whether you prefer your tea hot or cold, these recipes are sure to offer many new and irresistible creations.

ED'S TEA

Ecstasy is a glass full of tea and a piece of sugar in the mouth.

—ALEKSANDR PUSHKIN (1799–1837),
POET

YIELD: 8 SERVINGS

6 cups water

1 tablespoon whole cloves, or to taste

1 cinnamon stick

5 tea bags

2 cups orange juice, or to taste

Sweetener to taste (optional)

This recipe for iced tea makes a pitcher full of pleasure—and sugar is optional. Serve over ice in a tall glass, on a warm day, under the shade of a big tree, compliments of Ed. My dear friend Ed, a former police officer, has passed away, but I like to think of him keeping the peace above while sipping a heavenly cup of his favorite tea and resting comfortably in his beloved rock garden.

1. Place the water, cloves, and cinnamon in a two-quart pot.

2. Stir, cover, and let set for 15 to 30 minutes.

3. Place over medium heat and bring to a boil. Remove from heat, add tea, cover, and let steep for 10 minutes.

4. While tea steeps, place orange juice in a two-quart pitcher with lid. Stir in sweetener, if desired.

5. After tea has steeped, strain into an empty container or pitcher, adding orange juice to fill.

6. Tea can be served hot or cold. To serve cold, chill in refrigerator for one day to enhance the flavor. For hot tea, serve immediately.

ICY FRUIT TEA

*There is no denying the fruit juices in this irresistible
icy tea create a delicious combination.*

1. Place tea bags in a medium bowl and add boiling water.

2. Let steep for 10 minutes, then remove tea bags.

3. Add honey and mint and mix well.

4. Place orange juice, pineapple juice, and lime juice in a large container and stir.

5. Add tea mixture to the juice container and refrigerate until ready to use.

6. To serve, fill each glass with ice cubes. Add ½ cup of the tea-fruit juice mixture, and fill the remainder of the glass with carbonated water.

YIELD: 6 SERVINGS

4 tea bags

I cup boiling water

½ cup honey

¼ cup crumbled fresh mint leaves

I cup orange juice

¾ cup pineapple juice

¼ cup lime juice

I quart, plus 2 cups carbonated water

TEA SANGRIA

*Try this tea for a refreshing, non-alcoholic alternative to the popular,
treasured Spanish beverage, Sangria.*

1. In a teapot, pour boiling water over tea bags; cover and brew 5 minutes.

2. Remove tea bags and let cool.

3. In a large pitcher, combine fruit with sugar.

4. Pour tea over fruit and stir in the white grape juice.

5. Serve in ice-filled 10-ounce glasses.

YIELD: 6 SERVINGS

4 cups boiling water

5 English Breakfast tea bags

2 cups sliced fresh fruit*

2 tablespoons sugar

2 cups white grape juice

* Use any combination of apples, peaches, pineapple, oranges, or strawberries.

YIELD: **4** SERVINGS

8–12 ice cubes

16 ounces double-strength chai tea, cooled

4 ounces milk

2 ounces Torani orgeat (almond) syrup

2 ounces Torani coconut syrup

1 ounce Torani passionfruit syrup

1 ounce half-and-half

4 cinnamon sticks

DREAM SHIP'S THAI ICED TEA

America's most loved clown, Red Skelton, charmed audiences for twenty years with his weekly television show and signature sign off, "Goodnight and God bless." But how did he cheer himself? When others let him down, Skelton turned to tea. He once told The New York Times, *"When anyone hurts us, my wife and I sit in our Japanese garden and drink tea."*

If someone gives you the cold shoulder, soothe your spirit with quiet contemplation and this cool creation—a wonderful milky sweet drink served at Thai restaurants.

1. Combine all the ingredients in a blender.

2. Blend in short bursts on high until all the ice is chopped fine and the mix is even.

3. Pour into tall glasses and garnish each with a cinnamon stick.

YIELD: **1** SERVING

4 ounces ice

8 ounces Stash English or Irish Breakfast tea, brewed double strength

2 ounces coconut syrup

1 ounce cream or half-and-half

FIJI ICED TEA

On a hot day this cool, creamy coconut creation will quench your thirst and transport you to a tropical paradise.

1. Combine ice, tea, coconut syrup, and cream or half-and-half in a cocktail shaker or jar with a lid.

2. Shake until cold and frothy.

3. Pour into a tall iced tea glass.

SOUTHERN SWEET ICED TEA

It is said that half of all the iced tea in the United Stated is consumed in the South, where greeting guests with a refreshing glass of this beverage is a tradition. This recipe is for perfectly sweetened iced tea!

1. Bring water to a boil.

2. Add baking soda and tea bags to boiling water.

3. Remove from heat and cover for at least 10–15 minutes.

4. Pour into a gallon pitcher and add sugar.

5. Fill the pitcher with cold water and refrigerate.

YIELD: 16 SERVINGS

3–4 cups water

Pinch of baking soda (about ¼ teaspoon)

9 tea bags

1–1⅓ cups sugar

FESTIVE EGG NOG

This rich and satisfying recipe will be welcome at the holidays or any time of the year.

1. Brew tea bags in 1 cup of boiling water.

2. Steep for 5 minutes.

3. Remove tea bags and cool tea.

4. Add beaten eggs, condensed milk, vanilla, salt, and milk to the tea and mix well.

5. Serve in mugs garnished with whipping cream and ground nutmeg.

YIELD: 6 SERVINGS

6 Darjeeling or English Breakfast tea bags

1 cup (8 ounces) water

2 eggs, beaten

1 can (14 ounces) sweetened condensed milk

1 teaspoon vanilla extract

¼ teaspoon salt

1 quart milk

½ pint whipping cream

Ground nutmeg

ICE PICK TEA

YIELD: **1** SERVING

1 ½ ounces vodka

6 ounces iced tea,
prepared

Lemon juice to taste

*With a spike of vodka and a bit of lemon, this refreshing iced tea is a
great way to kick off your next celebration.*

1. Pour vodka in glass and fill with iced tea.

2. Stir in lemon to taste.

FROZEN FRUITY TEA PARTY PUNCH

YIELD: **16** SERVINGS

7 cups water

3 cups light rum

2 cups fruit-flavored
black tea (peach,
mango, or raspberry),
prepared

1 ½ cups sugar

12 ounces frozen
fruit punch

12 ounces frozen
pink lemonade

10 ounce jar
cherries with juice

Lemon-lime
carbonated beverage,
such as 7-Up
(optional)

*If you are anticipating a long evening, this slow-sipping
recipe is just the thing to keep the party going.*

1. Place all the ingredients (except the lemon-lime soda) in a large pitcher.
Mix everything together well, and place in the freezer.

2. When the mixture becomes slushy,
remove from freezer and drink
as is, or mix with the soda to taste.

ICED ANISEED TEA

YIELD: 4 SERVINGS

*The aniseed in this delicious drink brings a unique
richness to a classic iced tea recipe.*

1. Combine aniseed and 1 cup water in a saucepan and bring to a boil.

2. Simmer 5–10 minutes or until aniseed is tender.

3. Bring remaining 2 cups of water to a boil in another saucepan.

4. Add the tea leaves (or bags) to the 2 cups of boiling water and remove from heat. Steep 5–6 minutes or until the tea is very strong.

5. Strain tea into a large pitcher.

6. Strain liquid from aniseed into tea.

7. Stir in milk and sugar, or sweeten to taste. Chill and serve over ice.

3 tablespoons aniseed

3 cups water

I tablespoon plus
I teaspoon loose
black tea
or 4 tea bags,
tags removed

I cup milk

I tablespoon plus
I teaspoon sugar,
or to taste

Ice cubes

RASPBERRY TEA SMOOTHIE

YIELD: 4 SERVINGS

*This satisfying smoothie combines the pleasure of tea with the sweetness
of fruit for an irresistible creation you'll surely want to share.*

1. Steep tea bags in 1 cup boiling water for 5 minutes. Discard tea bags and cool.

2. Place tea, frozen raspberries, ice cubes, yogurt, and sugar in blender on liquefy setting; blend until smooth.

3. Pour into 4 tall glasses and serve.

4 raspberry-flavored
black tea bags

I cup boiling water

2 cups fresh or frozen
raspberries

6 ice cubes

2 containers (6 ounces
each) raspberry yogurt

$^1/_2$ cup sugar

YIELD: ABOUT 25
SERVICES

1 quart black tea,
prepared strong

1 quart rye whiskey

1 bottle red wine
(26 ounces)

1 pint Jamaica rum

1 pint orange juice

½ pint brandy

½ pint lemon juice

½ pint sugar syrup

1 ounce Benedictine
liqueur

Lemon peel

ARTILLERY PUNCH

*If I'd have stood off Naseem, there wouldn't have been a fight tonight.
I could've sat in the corner and had a cup of tea. How can you be a world
champion and run away? I don't say stand toe to toe, but at least come to me.*

—WAYNE MCCULLOUGH, BOXER, ON HIS 12-ROUND DEFEAT TO
WBO FEATHERWEIGHT CHAMPION PRINCE NASEEM HAMED
NOVEMBER 2, 1998

*After a bout with the then-undefeated champion Prince Hamed,
McCullough probably could have appreciated a refreshing cup of tea.
But you don't have to go toe-to-toe in a boxing ring to appreciate
the knockout flavor of this powerful punch.*

1. Place all the ingredients in a large punch bowl together with a block
of ice.

2. Garnish with twists of lemon peel.

LEMONY ICED TEA

YIELD: 6 SERVINGS

In June 1999, David Duval was ranked the number-one golfer in the world, and was a favorite to win the U.S. Open. Less than one week before the Open, he picked up a teapot from the gas stove in his new home. Unfortunately, the gas stove burned hotter than Duval's old electric one, and he received second-degree burns on his right thumb and forefinger.
Duval went on to play the Open anyway. He finished seventh.
Maybe it was the teapot; maybe it just wasn't his day.

Whether out for an afternoon of golf or puttering in the garden, if you are exposed to the sun, drink plenty of liquids—cold liquids. Iced tea is a delicious way to fill up on fluids, and this lemony libation has a taste that's easy to appreciate.

4 cups plus 1 cup water

5 lemon-flavored black tea bags

$\frac{1}{2}$ cup sugar

1 cup lemon juice

1. Bring 4 cups of water to a boil and remove from heat.

2. Add tea bags and steep for 5 minutes; discard tea bags.

3. Stir in sugar until it dissolves; add lemon juice and remaining cup of water.

4. Chill and serve over ice.

YIELD: 12 OUNCES OF CONCENTRATE

16 ounces water

2 chai tea bags

AUBREY'S CHAI TEA CONCENTRATE

The Aubrey here is Sir Aubrey, of Sir Aubrey Tea Company fame.
Use this concentrate in the recipe below for Iced Chai Latte.

1. Bring water to a boil and add the chai tea bags.

2. Steep for 7 minutes. Remove tea bags.

3. Cover and chill the concentrate until cold, for at least 3 hours and up to 2 weeks.

YIELD: 2 SERVINGS

½ cup milk

½ cup half-and-half

1 tablespoon sugar

6 whole cardamom pods, crushed

12 ounces chai tea concentrate, chilled (see recipe above for *Aubrey's Chai Tea Concentrate*)

ICED CHAI LATTE

This wonderful recipe combines the richness of chai with a cool
and creamy iced tea brew that's perfect for a hot summer day.

1. In saucepan, stir together milk, half-and-half, sugar, and cardamom pods.

2. Bring mixture to boil, stirring until sugar is dissolved, and let cool.

3. Strain mixture through sieve.

4. Stir in chai tea concentrate and chill mixture, covered, for 20 minutes or until cold.

5. Divide iced latte between 2 glasses filled with ice cubes.

VARIATION

Serve with a splash of brandy or Kahlua.

IRRESISTIBLE ICE CREAM TEA

If you love tea and ice cream, what could be better than a cup full of both? Try this simple recipe for an "irresistible" treat.

1. Bring water to a boil over high heat.

2. Place the tea bags in a medium bowl and add boiling water.

3. Let stand 4 minutes and remove tea bags.

4. Add ice cream and stir until melted.

5. Refrigerate until chilled.

6. To serve, pour over ice-filled glasses.

YIELD: 2 SERVINGS

3 cups water

2 chai or black tea bags

2 large scoops
vanilla ice cream

Ice cubes

MEXICAN TEA PUNCH

This spirited punch is a delicious, thirst-quenching combination of tea, tequila, and fruit juices.

1. Place all ingredients in a large pitcher; mix well.

2. Refrigerate until chilled.

3. Stir before serving over ice.

YIELD: 6 SERVINGS

2 cups tequila

2 cups tea, prepared
strong and chilled

1 cup pineapple juice

1/4 cup cold water

1/4 cup lemon juice

1/4 cup honey

1/4 cup lime juice

1 1/2 teaspoons
aromatic bitters

1 1/2 teaspoons ground
cinnamon

SUN TEA

YIELD: **1** GALLON

9 tea bags

1 gallon water

Ice cubes

Sweetener to taste

*This classic warm-weather tea is a perfect refresher for the
end of a long summer day. And don't forget that the tea bags,
once cooled, can offer soothing relief when applied to
sunburned skin.*

1. Put the tea bags in a clean gallon jar and fill with fresh, cold water.

2. Cap loosely and place in the hot sunshine for 3–4 hours.

3. Remove tea bags.

4. Refrigerate within 5 hours of brewing until chilled.

5. Serve over ice and sweeten to taste.

VARIATION

Vary the number of tea bags and the duration of brewing according
to the tea strength you desire. For a delicious change of taste, add
3 bags of orange spice tea.

BOSTON TEA HARDY

YIELD: **1** SERVING

**3 ounces iced tea,
prepared**

1 1/4 ounces dark rum

3 ounces orange juice

Orange slice

Mint sprig

*This spirited iced tea is spiked with rum
and sweetened with orange juice.*

1. Place the iced tea, rum, and orange juice in a cocktail shaker.
Shake ingredients together with ice.

2. Strain over ice cubes into a highball glass.

3. Garnish with an orange slice and a mint sprig.

STRAWBERRY LEMONADE ICED TEA

YIELD: 8 SERVINGS

*By now, you've most likely read about the amazing health benefits
of drinking green tea. However, if you still hesitate to give up your
black tea for green, give this deliciously sweet iced tea recipe a try.
Its delightful combination of green tea, strawberries,
and lemonade is difficult to resist.*

4 cups boiling water
plus 3 cups water

4 green tea bags

1 can (12 ounces)
frozen lemonade
concentrate

2 cups frozen
strawberries

1. Bring 4 cups of water to a boil and remove from heat. Steep tea bags for 5 minutes; discard bags and set aside the tea.

2. Put the lemonade concentrate, strawberries, and 3 cups of water in a blender and blend on medium until smooth.

3. In a gallon container, stir together tea and blended lemonade-strawberry mixture. Chill and serve over ice.

SMOOTH TICKLE TEA

YIELD: 1 SERVING

"I drink tea when I work like rummies drink beer."

—ERNEST HEMINGWAY, 1952 LETTER TO HARVEY BREIT

*Combine the two and you'll have a delicious duo—
a perfect reward at the end of a hard day's work!*

¼ pint iced tea,
prepared

Sugar to taste

¾ pint beer

1. Pour iced tea into a pint glass.

2. Add sugar until you feel it tastes way too sweet.

3. Add beer and stir gently until the sugar is no longer sitting on the bottom of the glass.

4. Bottoms up!

SPEARMINT TEA

YIELD: 4 SERVINGS

2 teaspoons Gunpowder tea

I handful fresh spearmint

2 tablespoons sugar

3 ½ cups boiling water

Lemon slices for garnish

Fresh mint sprigs for garnish

After two months of traveling alone on foot, Norwegian adventurer Boerge Ousland was nearing the end of his historic, record-breaking 1,675-mile trek across Antarctica. Challenged by snowstorms, freezing temperatures, and deadly crevasses, Ousland was on the last leg of his long journey. According to an Associated Press article, Ousland, approaching New Zealand's Scott Base, sent word ahead conveying his first desire, of which Julian Tangaer (leader of Scott Base) is quoted as reporting: "A message has been relayed to us that the first thing he wants is a cup of tea."

If there's nothing you'd enjoy more than a hot cup of tea, try this soothing creation.

1. Rinse teapot with boiling water

2. Place tea, spearmint, and sugar in teapot.

3. Cover with fresh boiling water and brew for 5 minutes.

4. Strain into cups; garnish with lemon and a fresh sprig of mint, if desired.

HEARTH-WARMING TEA

YIELD: **7** SERVINGS

*While any black tea can be used here, why not use
the Earl's own blend—Earl Grey, that is—to prepare
this sweet-spiced, Hearth-Warming tea.*

1. Bring cranberry juice, orange juice, and water to a boil.

2. Add brown sugar, cinnamon, and cloves and simmer 20 minutes.

3. Remove from heat and add tea bags.

4. Cover and steep 10 minutes. Remove tea bags.

5. Serve hot or iced.

2 cups cranberry juice

1 cup orange juice

4 cups cold water

$3/4$ cup brown sugar

1 teaspoon ground cinnamon

$1/2$ teaspoon ground cloves

4 black tea bags

QUIET TIME TEA

YIELD: **60** SERVINGS

*This relaxing blend is a great way to end a hectic day.
Use just 1 teaspoon per serving and then store the rest
in an airtight container in a cool, dry place for later use.*

1. Crush herbs before measuring; mix well.

2. Mix 1 teaspoon of herbs with 1 cup boiling water.

3. Steep for at least 5 minutes.

4. Store unused herb mixture in an airtight container in a cool, dry place.

1 cup dried strawberry leaves

$1/2$ cup dried catnip leaves

$1/4$ cup dried chamomile

$1/4$ cup dried thyme

YIELD: 4 SERVINGS

8 English Breakfast or
Irish Breakfast tea bags

4 cups water

3 whole cloves

$1/4$ teaspoon fennel
seeds

$1/4$ teaspoon ground
cardamom

$1/2$ teaspoon ground
ginger

$1/2$ pint half-and-half
or condensed milk

Honey or sugar
to taste

CHAI BLEND

This richly spiced tea is the traditional drink of India.
Once you try a cup of this delicious brew, you'll understand why.

1. Bring the water to a boil in a saucepan. Add the tea bags, and remove from the heat.

2. Steep tea for 5 minutes.

3. Remove tea bags.

4. Add cloves, fennel, cardamom, and ginger and simmer for 10 minutes.

5. Add half-and-half or milk, and sweeten to taste.

CALMING SPIRIT TEA BLEND

YIELD: **120** SERVINGS

1 cup dried rosemary

1 cup dried lavender flowers

1 cup dried spearmint leaves

$^1/_2$ cup dried chamomile

$^1/_4$ to $^1/_2$ cup dried cloves

In 1773, Samuel Adams, Paul Revere, and other tax-tired colonists dumped tea into Boston Harbor. In 1775, in a symbolic gesture to support the Boston Tea Party and show their contempt for British tyranny, Providence citizens marched on Market House—the center of the city's marketplace and government—and destroyed bales of herbs.

Instead of destroying the bales of herbs, maybe the angry citizens of Rhode Island should have steeped them in a cup of tea. This calming cuppa is created with a collection of soothing herbs.

1. Blend all herbs thoroughly.

2. Add 1 cup of boiling water to 1 teaspoon of herbs.

3. Steep about 5 minutes and strain.

4. Store the remaining tea mixture in an airtight container in a cool, dry place.

VARIATION

For a special treat, place a handful of this herbal mixture in a muslin bag and add to a bath for a soothing soak.

YIELD: **30** SERVINGS

¹/₂ cup instant tea, unsweetened

8 ounces powdered orange drink (like Tang)

¹/₃ cup sugar

1 teaspoon ground cinnamon

1 teaspoon dried cloves

RUSSIAN TEA

This is a modern spin on a classic tea recipe. Some may dislike its powdered tea component, but I'd venture a guess that its sweet simplicity ensures it will be around for years to come.

1. Mix all ingredients together and keep in an airtight container.

2. Use approximately 3 heaping teaspoons per 1 cup of tea.

3. Add hot water and adjust to taste. Serve hot or iced.

YIELD: **2** SERVINGS

2 cups water

1 tablespoon honey

4 lemon slices

4 cinnamon sticks, broken into small pieces

4 tea bags

Lemon slices for garnish (optional)

LEMON SPICE TEA

The comfort of a cup of tea is universal. But if it's difficult to find time in your busy day to relax with a cuppa, maybe you just need to be lured to the teapot with a special brew, such as Lemon Spice Tea.

1. Combine water, honey, lemon slices, and cinnamon in a saucepan over high heat.

2. Bring to a boil. Add the tea bags, and remove from heat.

3. Cover and steep for 4 minutes.

4. Remove the tea bags and lemons slices, and use a strainer to remove the cinnamon pieces.

5. Pour into two mugs and garnish with additional lemon slices, if desired.

DIGESTIVE TEA

YIELD: **30** SERVINGS

If you're seeking a way to soothe an upset stomach,
try a cup of this soothing herbal blend.

1. Blend all herbs thoroughly.

2. Use 1 teaspoon of the herb mixture to make 1 cup of tea.

3. For each serving, mix 1 teaspoon of the herbs plus 1 cup boiling water. Steep for about 5 minutes.

4. Store unused herb mixture in an airtight container in a cool, dry place.

1/4 cup dried mint

1/4 cup lemon verbena

2 tablespoons dried thyme

2 tablespoons dried rosemary

2 tablespoons aniseed

CROCKPOT TROPICAL TEA WARMER

YIELD: **10** SERVINGS

This warm and wonderful recipe is best made using a crockpot,
and is perfect for sharing with friends and family.

1. Warm your crockpot first with hot tap water.

2. In a saucepan over high heat, bring 6 cups of water to boiling. Pour over tea bags in the crockpot.

3. Cover and let steep for 5 minutes.

4. Remove tea bags and stir in sugar, honey, orange juice, pineapple juice, and orange slices.

5. Cover and heat on low for 2 to 3 hours; serve from crockpot.

6 cups water

6 tea bags

1/3 cup sugar

2 tablespoons honey

1 1/2 cups orange juice

1 1/2 cups pineapple juice

1 orange, sliced (unpeeled)

YIELD: 8 SERVINGS

5 cups water

2 teaspoons grated
fresh ginger

2 teaspoons grated
orange peel

1 teaspoon grated
lemon peel

2 cinnamon sticks,
broken in half

2 chai tea bags

1/4 cup honey

1 1/2 cups milk

1 1/2 cups whipped
cream

1 teaspoon vanilla

CHAI NOG

*"There is a subtle charm in the taste of tea which makes it irresistible and
capable of idealization. Western humorists were not slow to mingle the
fragrance of their thought with its aroma. It has not the arrogance of wine,
the self-consciousness of coffee, nor the simpering innocence of cocoa."*

—KAKUZO OKAKURA
THE BOOK OF TEA

*This Chai Nog offers a delicious alternative to traditional holiday
eggnog. But feel free to enjoy this creation anytime you choose!*

1. In saucepan, bring water, ginger, orange and lemon peel, and cinnamon to a boil.

2. Add tea bags, remove from heat, and steep for 7 minutes.

3. Add honey, milk, cream, and vanilla to the tea.

4. To serve hot, reheat liquid over medium heat; to serve cold, pour over crushed ice.

YIELD: 6 SERVINGS

3 cups water

4 tea bags

1/3 cup honey

3 cups unsweetened
apple juice

Lemon slices

HONEY APPLE TEA

*If your friend is enjoying a cup of this sweet sensation,
it would be difficult not to desire a taste.*

1. In a two-quart pot, bring water to a boil. Remove from heat, add tea bags, and steep tea for 5 minutes.

2. Remove tea bags; add honey and apple juice and simmer until hot.

3. Ladle into cups and garnish with lemon slices.

CHOCOLATE MINT TEA

Love and scandal are the best sweeteners of tea

—HENRY FIELDING (1707–1754)

1. Place tea bags in bottom of pan.
2. Add milk and heat to just under boiling.
3. Remove tea bags.
4. Place 1 tablespoon of chocolate mix in each mug.
5. Pour one cup of hot minted milk over chocolate.
6. Serve with fresh mint leaf or peppermint stick candy.

YIELD: 6 SERVINGS

5 peppermint tea bags

6 cups (48 ounces) milk

6 tablespoons hot chocolate mix

Fresh mint leaf (optional)

Peppermint stick candy (optional)

SPICY TEA

This delightful blend of herbs makes a delicious cup of tea and provides a perfect excuse to take a break any time of day.

1. Blend together the lemon verbena, chamomile, orange peel, rosemary, and cinnamon thoroughly.
2. Place 1 teaspoon in a cup or mug and fill with 1 cup boiling water. Steep for about 5 minutes.
3. Served hot or chilled as iced tea.
4. Store the remaining herb mixture in an airtight container in a cool, dry place.

YIELD: 30 SERVINGS

1/4 cup dried lemon verbena

1/4 cup dried chamomile

1/4 cup dried orange peel

2 tablespoons dried rosemary

1 cinnamon stick (about 3 inches), crushed

HOT SPICED TEA WITH MILK

YIELD: 6 SERVINGS

1 quart plus 2 cups water

¼ teaspoon ground cloves

1 cinnamon stick

1 tablespoon loose black tea

1 cup milk, heated

4 teaspoons sugar, or to taste

*The charm of a pleasing cup of tea is known to good and evil alike.
One of the most evil men to walk the earth
was nearly brought down with a simple cup of tea.
During World War II, Britain's Special Operations Executive (SOE)
launched "Operation Foxely"—an initiative to assassinate Adolph
Hitler. Along with the usual messy options of bombing the fuhrer's car
or shooting him, the SOE came up with a particularly inventive idea
to poison him with anthrax, a lethal bacteria.
The deadly deed was to be carried out by a French maid
as Hitler traveled on his private train. According to the plan,
she was to slip a tiny bit of anthrax along with some milk into his tea.
(The milk would serve as the perfect disguise.)
But as the success of the Allies grew and Hitler's forces faltered,
the SOE believed he was more valuable to the Allies alive
than dead, so the operation was cancelled in April of 1945.
Hitler killed himself a few days later on April 30.*

1. Bring water, cloves, and cinnamon stick to a boil.

2. Remove from heat and add tea.

3. Cover and let steep for 4 minutes, or longer if stronger tea is desired.

4. Strain tea.

5. Stir in hot milk and sugar to taste.

CHAPTER 7

CookingWithTea

I care not a jot for immortal life,
but only for the taste of tea.

—LU TUNG (C. EIGHTH CENTURY)
CHINESE POET

Tea makes everything tastier! Although you know about beverages, you may not have ever thought of using tea as an ingredient for food recipes. As this chapter will show, however, delicious options await when you start cooking with tea. Don't hesitate to use tea for meals, including dinner's main course and side dishes. Treat yourself to these scrumptious tea-laced desserts. Spice up poultry, seafood, vegetarian dishes, marinades—the possibilities are endless. Remember—when recipes do not call for a specific type of tea, feel free to use your favorite. It's time to take a fresh look at the traditional elixir, because tea is definitely not just for sipping.

TEA TREATS

CHAI TIRAMISU

"Its liquor is like the sweetest dew from heaven."

—LU YU, *THE CLASSIC OF TEA*

YIELD: 6 SERVINGS

20 ounces cream cheese

6 tablespoons sugar

4 egg yolks

1/2 cup espresso

1 cup Oregon Chai Original Chai concentrate

1/2 cup coffee liqueur

2 ounces rum

1/2 teaspoon nutmeg

12 ladyfingers

6 ounces semi-sweet chocolate chips

1. Beat cream cheese, sugar, and egg yolks until smooth.

2. In a microwave, heat espresso, Original Chai concentrate, coffee liqueur, rum, and nutmeg until just warm.

3. Add the ladyfingers and soak in the coffee-chai mix.

4. Finely chop or grind chocolate chips using pulse setting on food processor or blender.

5. Line a 9-x-5-inch loaf pan with plastic wrap.

6. Place 1/2 the ladyfingers on the bottom and up the sides of pan.

7. Sprinkle with 1/3 of the ground chocolate and 1/2 of the cream cheese mixture.

8. Add a layer of ladyfingers (using 1/2 of the remaining amount) over cream cheese mix.

9. Add another layer of 1/3 chocolate and the rest of the cream cheese mixture.

10. Layer the remaining ladyfingers on top.

11. Refrigerate 12 hours; remove from the pan. Sprinkle with remaining chocolate chips.

MANGO PASSIONFRUIT CHEESECAKE

"There are few hours in life more agreeable than the hour dedicated to the ceremony known as afternoon tea."

—HENRY JAMES (1843–1916)

American writer James became a British subject in 1915, which just might explain his fondness for afternoon tea. This terrific cheesecake recipe would be an admirable accompaniment to any cup of tea.

1. Preheat oven to 350° F.

2. In large bowl, combine the contents of tea bags, cream cheese, and sugar. Mix well with an electric mixer.

3. Add eggs and blend until smooth.

4. Pour into pie crust and bake at 350° F for 40 minutes.

5. Cool in refrigerator at least 3 hours.

YIELD: 9-INCH CHEESECAKE

6 Stash Tea Mango Passionfruit tea bags

2 containers (8 ounces each) regular or fat-free cream cheese, softened

$\frac{1}{2}$ cup sugar

2 eggs

9-inch (6-ounce) graham cracker pie crust

TEA GLAZE

This slightly sweet, easy-to-make glaze is the perfect topping for many desserts, breads, and pastries, including Tea Scones, which can be found on page 136.

1. Brew the tea bags in the boiling water for 5 minutes.

2. Remove tea bags, then stir in 2 tablespoons sugar and let cool.

3. Serve as a glaze coating to *Tea Scones*, or other creations.

YIELD: ENOUGH TO COAT 8 SCONES

2 Lipton Flo-Thru tea bags

$\frac{1}{2}$ cup boiling water

2 tablespoons sugar

2 cups all purpose
flour

2 teaspoons baking
powder

¼ cup sugar

½ teaspoon salt

4 tablespoons cold
butter, cut into pieces

½ cup milk

3 Lipton Flo-Thru
regular or
decaffeinated tea bags

1 egg, beaten

Tea Glaze (page 135)

Honey (optional)

TEA SCONES

"First you have tea, then you can look in the mirror."

—DR. LAURA SCHLESSINGER

People just don't drink tea to relax. Some—myself included—depend on it to get going in the morning. Unless it specifies decaffeinated, all tea contains caffeine, although a cup of tea has significantly less caffeine than a cup of coffee—about one third to one half. This means that tea drinkers get to enjoy their beverage of choice long after our coffee-drinking cohorts have reached their limit. These Tea Scones are the perfect complement to a morning (or afternoon) cup of tea.

1. Preheat oven to 400° F.

2. In medium bowl, combine flour, baking powder, sugar, and salt.

3. With pastry blender or fingers, cut or rub in butter until mixture is the size of small peas; set aside.

4. In small saucepan, bring milk to the boiling point. Add tea bags; cover and brew 5 minutes. Remove tea bags; cool.

5. Beat in egg.

6. Gradually add tea mixture to flour mixture, stirring until just combined.

7. Line a cookie sheet with flour. Pour mixture onto cookie sheet and pat into an 8-inch circle.

8. With the blunt edge of a knife, score (lightly cut) the top of the dough into 8 pre-shaped wedges.

9. Brush with Tea Glaze (see page 135) and bake 20 minutes or until golden brown.

10. Let cool on wire rack. Serve with honey, if desired.

IRISH TEA BREAD

YIELD: 4 SERVINGS

Next to water, tea is the most consumed beverage in the world. But who are the world's biggest tea drinkers? The British? No. Although the Tea Council of the United Kingdom estimates three quarters of the British population over the age of ten drink tea every day, the world's biggest tea drinkers are the Irish. According to the International Tea Committee, in 2001 the Irish consumed an average of 5.9 pounds per person annually—compared to 5 pounds per person in England and only 0.72 pounds per person in the United States. Each pound equals about 200 servings of tea.

1 pound mixed dried fruit*

12 tablespoons strong tea

6 ounces brown sugar

1 egg, lightly beaten

1 ounce butter, melted

9 ounces all purpose flour

$1/2$ teaspoon baking soda

*The mixed fruit can include raisins, currants, and any other dried fruit you like.

1. Chop any larger pieces of dried fruit to about raisin size.

2. Place the tea, mixed fruit, and sugar in a bowl; cover and leave overnight.

3. Preheat oven to 350° F.

4. Stir the egg and butter into the fruit mixture.

5. Sift together the flour and baking soda, and fold into the mixture.

6. Line the bottom of a large loaf pan with baking parchment, and brush the entire pan with melted butter.

7. Pour the mixture in and smooth the top.

8. Bake in preheated oven on the middle shelf for $1^1/2$ hours.

9. After removing from the oven, let the bread sit in the pan for 2–3 minutes. Remove from the pan and cool on wire rack.

PUMPKIN CHAI PIE

YIELD: 9-INCH PIE

1 can (15 ounces) pumpkin

1 teaspoon ground cinnamon

1/2 teaspoon ground ginger

1/2 teaspoon ground nutmeg

3/4 cup sugar

3 eggs

2/3 cup evaporated milk

1/2 cup Celestial Seasonings Mountain Chai concentrate (any flavor)

Single 9-inch pie crust

Whipped cream

The best tea is even better when served with a tasty treat, like this wonderful chai pie.

1. Preheat oven to 375° F.

2. Blend pumpkin, cinnamon, ginger, nutmeg, and sugar in a mixing bowl.

3. Beat eggs with a fork and add to pumpkin mixture.

4. Add evaporated milk and Mountain Chai and mix well.

5. Pour mixture into pie crust.

6. Cover edges of pie crust with foil.

7. Bake for 25 minutes.

8. Remove foil and bake for 25–35 minutes more, or until a knife, inserted into the center, comes out clean.

9. Cool. Top with whipped cream and serve. Cover and chill to store.

COCONUTEA COOKIES

YIELD: 30 COOKIES

*Americans consume over 2 billion gallons of tea a year and more than
60 percent of it is prepared using tea bags. While tea bags are popularly
used for brewing cups of tea, more and more they are being used in
cooking. This cookie recipe is an excellent
example of how, rather than brewing your tea with a bag,
you might try baking with it instead.*

1. Preheat oven to 350° F.

2. In teapot, pour boiling water over tea bags; cover and steep
   5 minutes. Cool.

3. In small bowl, combine flour, baking powder, baking soda, and salt;
   set aside.

4. With an electric mixer, beat butter and sugars until well-blended.

5. Add egg, vanilla, and tea until just blended.

6. At low speed, gradually beat in flour mixture.

7. Stir in 1 cup coconut.

8. On greased cookie sheet, drop mixture by tablespoons.
   Sprinkle with remaining ¼ cup coconut.

9. Bake 12 minutes or until golden.

10. Cool slightly; remove from cookie sheet and
    let cool completely on wire rack.

½ cup boiling water

2 Lipton Flo-Thru
tea bags

1 ¾ cups all purpose
flour

½ teaspoon baking
powder

½ teaspoon baking
soda

½ teaspoon salt

12 tablespoons butter,
softened

½ cup light brown
sugar

⅓ cup sugar

1 egg

½ teaspoon vanilla
extract

1 ¼ cups shredded
coconut

CINNAMON-ORANGE SPICE TEA SOUFFLÉ GLACÉ

YIELD: 25 SERVINGS

25 Läderach Dark
Chocolate Soufflé
Cups*

5 ounces water

I ounce Cinnamon
Orange Spice Tea

10 egg yolks

9 ounces sugar

3 egg whites

21 ounces heavy
cream, whipped

*These Swiss chocolate
cups can be ordered
through Albert Uster
Imports (see *Resource List*).
You may substitute with
similar products found at
gourmet shops and upscale
grocery stores.

*This gourmet treat blends the richness of dark chocolate
and delicious spices with a creamy meringue
for an unforgettable cool combination.*

1. Surround each dark chocolate soufflé cup with aluminum foil to create a mold.

2. Bring water to a boil.

3. Add tea leaves and let infuse for about a half hour.

4. Strain to remove the tea leaves and set aside.

5. Combine the egg yolks and half the sugar and whip at high speed until light.

6. Prepare meringue with egg whites and remaining sugar.

7. Combine light egg yolk-sugar mixture with tea infusion.

8. Fold in meringue and prepared whipped cream.

9. Pour the mixture in prepared chocolate soufflé cups and place in freezer for several hours.

APRICOT TEA BREAD

*You won't be able to resist a slice of this slightly sweet bread.
Its wonderful combination of fruit and rich maple syrup
makes it a perfect complement to a warm cup of tea.*

1. Preheat oven to 350° F.

2. Soak apricots for 20 minutes in tea.

3. Mix together flour, baking powder, and baking soda.

4. In another bowl, beat maple syrup, butter, and egg.

5. Drain tea from apricots into the mandarin orange syrup.

6. Stir flour into butter mixture a little at a time, alternating with syrup mixture.

7. Stir in apricots and nuts.

8. Pour batter into lightly oiled 9-x-5-inch loaf pan.

9. Bake for 45–60 minutes. Bread will be golden brown, and a toothpick inserted in the center will come out clean when finished.

10. Let cool before slicing and serve.

YIELD: 1 LOAF

$1/2$ cup packed, dried apricots

$1/3$ cup double-strength apricot tea

2 cups pastry flour

1 tablespoon baking powder

$1/4$ teaspoon baking soda

$1/2$ cup maple syrup

2 tablespoons butter

1 egg

$1/3$ cup Torani Mandarin Orange Syrup

$3/4$ cup chopped pecans

CHAI STICKY BUNS

YIELD: **12** SERVINGS

I cup Oregon Chai
Original Chai
concentrate

3/4 cup whole or
slightly chopped
pecans

1/4 cup raisins
(optional)

I puff pastry sheet
(9-x-10 inches)*

I tablespoon butter,
melted

1/2 teaspoon
cinnamon

1/3 cup brown sugar

1/3 cup honey

*These are usually available
frozen, 2 sheets per box.

Cinnamon buns are one of my favorite treats, and those made with this recipe are even better! Add delicious, rich chai to warm, buttery cinnamon, and you've got an unbeatable combination of temptingly sweet proportions!

1. Preheat oven to 375° F.

2. In a saucepan over high heat, bring Original Chai concentrate to a boil.

3. Reduce heat to medium and cook 25 minutes, or until reduced to half.

4. Combine pecans with 1/4 of reduced chai concentrate and set aside.

5. Combine raisins with 1 tablespoon of chai concentrate and set aside.

6. Brush pastry sheet with melted butter and sprinkle with cinnamon and raisins.

7. Roll into a log and chill 30 minutes.

8. Grease muffin tin.

9. Drain pecans and evenly divide between cups.

10. Divide brown sugar and honey between muffin cups.

11. Cut log into 12 pieces.

12. Place one piece over each sweet-ened pecan layer and flatten.

13. Bake at 375° for 20 minutes.

14. Remove from oven and brush buns with remaining chai concentrate.

15. Turn muffin tin onto buttered baking dish to release buns.

16. Cool slightly before serving.

CINNAMON BAKED APPLES

These yummy baked apples will fill your kitchen with the sweet smell of cinnamon. The use of tea is a nice addition to this traditional comfort food.

1. Preheat oven to 350° F.

2. In small saucepan, bring water to boil. Remove from heat and add tea bags; cover and steep 5 minutes. Remove tea bags and squeeze; set aside.

3. Peel top ⅓ of apples.

4. In 8-inch square baking dish, arrange apples.

5. In small bowl, combine sugar, walnuts, and raisins.

6. Fill each apple with walnut mixture and top with 1 teaspoon butter.

7. Pour tea over and around apples.

8. Bake uncovered, basting occasionally, for 1 hour or until apples are tender.

9. Just before serving, pour cream over apples, if desired.

YIELD: 4 SERVINGS

I cup water

4 Lipton Soothing Moments Cinnamon Apple Herbal Tea Bags

4 large cored baking apples, such as Rome or Golden Delicious

¼ cup dark brown sugar, firmly packed

¼ cup chopped walnuts

2 tablespoons raisins

4 teaspoons butter

¼ cup whipping or heavy cream (optional)

YIELD: 30 COOKIES

1 cup white sugar

3/4 cup vegetable oil

1/2 cup milk

2 eggs

3/4 teaspoon baking powder

1/2 teaspoon vanilla extract

3 2/3 cups all purpose flour

1 cup peach or apricot preserves

1/2 cup chopped almonds

3 ounces cream cheese, softened

2 tablespoons instant tea powder

2 1/2 teaspoons peach, apricot, or regular brandy

3/4 teaspoon ground cinnamon

Red and orange sugar

AUSTRIAN PEACH COOKIES

If you enjoy your favorite tea with a particular kind of food, chances are you're partaking in a new tea trend called "pairing." The Tea Council of the United Kingdom reports, just as wine can enhance the flavor of food, so can tea. Tea pairing, then, is simply a way of partnering food, wine, and liqueurs with its most complementary tea counterpart. For example, according to the Tea Council, Ceylon is best with mature cheddar and fine dessert wine, while Kenya is better matched with Austrian smoked cheese and Drambuie. Darjeeling is more suited to cream, such as cream cheese and cream desserts. Serve Earl Grey if you're making a ham and mustard sandwich or pampering yourself with crème brulée. And Assam is a wonderful complement to rich chocolatey desserts. You get the idea. Experiment with your own tea pairings. With nearly 3,000 varieties of tea in the world, there are endless opportunities to please your palate. Perhaps these delightful cookies are a good way to start.

1. Preheat oven to 350° F.

2. Combine sugar, oil, milk, eggs, baking powder, and vanilla in a large bowl.

3. Blend in enough flour to form a soft dough.

4. Roll into walnut-sized balls and place on ungreased cookie sheets.

5. Bake 15–20 minutes. Cookies will be pale. Remove; place on rack and cool.

6. Hollow out cookie center and reserve crumbs.

7. Combine the crumbs, preserves, almonds, cream cheese, instant tea powder, brandy, and cinnamon. Mix to blend.

8. Fill cookies with crumb mixture.

9. Press 2 cookies together to form a peach.

10. Brush lightly with brandy or water and dip one spot of the cookie in the red sugar for blush, and roll entire cookie in orange sugar.

11. If desired, top each cookie with an icing leaf. (You can also purchase plastic leaves for decoration.)

NUTCRACKER SWEET PIE

*From teapot to tabletop, this recipe will have guests
cheering its sweet virtues.*

1. Preheat oven to 350° F.

2. In a saucepan, steep the tea bags in boiling water for 4 minutes.

3. Remove and discard the tea bags.

4. Lower the heat to simmer.

5. Add chocolate and butter, stirring until melted.

6. Remove from the heat and let the mixture cool 10 minutes.

7. Add sugar, salt, nuts, and eggs and mix well.

8. Pour this mixture into a pie shell.

9. Bake in preheated oven for 45 minutes.

10. Serve warm or cool with whipped topping, if desired.

YIELD: 9-INCH PIE

2 Celestial Seasonings Nutcracker Sweet tea bags

1 cup boiling water

2 ounces unsweetened chocolate

$\frac{1}{3}$ cup butter

1 $\frac{1}{2}$ cups sugar

$\frac{1}{2}$ teaspoon salt

1 cup chopped mixed (unsalted) nuts

2 eggs

1 (9-inch) pie crust

Whipped topping (optional)

GINGER TEA PEAR CRISP

YIELD: 8 SERVINGS

1 cup boiling water

3 Lipton Flo-Thru tea bags

1 1/3 cups sugar

6 large pears, peeled, cored, and thinly sliced

2 tablespoons lemon juice

1/2 cup light brown sugar

1/2 cup all purpose flour

1/4 teaspoon ground cinnamon

6 tablespoons cold butter, cut in pieces

1/2 cup coarsely crushed gingersnap cookies (about 7 cookies)

1/2 cup chopped pecans or walnuts

2 tablespoons cornstarch

1 tablespoon water

Eat your fruits and vegetables—five servings a day, we're told. If you find that hard to swallow, try tea. Although not a substitute for fruits and vegetables, according to scientists at the U.S. Department of Agriculture, a cup of tea brewed for three to five minutes contains more antioxidants than one serving of twenty-two different kinds of fruits and vegetables, including apples, orange juice, garlic, onions, carrots, and broccoli. Luckily, tea and fruit are perfectly paired in this crunchy Ginger Tea Pear Crisp.

1. Preheat oven to 350° F.

2. In teapot, pour boiling water over tea bags; cover and brew 5 minutes. Remove tea bags.

3. In 5-quart saucepot, combine tea, sugar, pears, and lemon juice.

4. Bring to boil, then reduce heat to low and simmer 8 minutes or until pears are tender.

5. Remove pears, reserving 1 1/3 cups tea liquid.

6. In bottom of 2-quart shallow baking dish, arrange pears; set aside.

7. In medium bowl, combine brown sugar, flour, and cinnamon.

8. With pastry blender or fingers, cut or rub in butter until mixture is size of small peas. Stir in cookie crumbs and nuts; set aside.

9. In small saucepan, mix reserved tea liquid with cornstarch blended with 1 tablespoon water. Bring to boil, and continue boiling 1 minute, stirring constantly.

10. Pour over pears. Top pears with cookie crumb mixture.

11. Bake 30 minutes or until bubbling and golden brown.

CHAI MERINGUES

YIELD: 24 MERINGUES

*It's one thing when [negative] thoughts pop in your head,
it's another thing when we serve them tea and cookies.*

—DR. LAURA SCHLESSINGER

*Your guests will have only positive thoughts when you serve
these delightful, melt-in-your-mouth Chai Meringues.*

3 egg whites

1 cup granulated sugar

½ teaspoon cardamom

¼ teaspoon cinnamon

¼ teaspoon ground cloves

1. Preheat oven to 250° F.

2. Beat the egg whites with an electric mixer at low speed until they get foamy, then at high speed until they form stiff peaks. You should be able to turn the bowl sideways without the egg whites moving. Your bowl and beaters must be grease-free for this to work properly!

3. Gradually add sugar, a little at a time, while beating at high speed.

4. When all sugar has been beaten in, the egg whites will look shiny.

5. Add the spices and beat in as briefly as possible.

6. Drop the mixture into small mounds on baking sheets that have been covered with foil or parchment paper.

7. Bake for 90 minutes. Turn off the oven and leave the meringues to sit. Don't open the oven door!

8. Let them sit overnight (preferable) or at least until the oven cools. Remove from foil and serve. Store in an airtight container.

YIELD: **10** SERVINGS

I cup boiling water

2 Lipton Flo-Thru
tea bags

I large tart apple,
peeled, cored, and
coarsely chopped

I cup plus 2
tablespoons sugar

2 cups all purpose
flour

$^1/_2$ teaspoon baking
powder

$^1/_2$ teaspoon baking
soda

12 tablespoons butter,
softened

2 eggs

$^1/_2$ cup sour cream

I teaspoon vanilla
extract

*Apple Crumb
Topping*

$^1/_2$ cup light brown
sugar

$^1/_3$ cup all purpose flour

$^1/_2$ teaspoon ground
cinnamon

APPLE TEA COFFEE CAKE

*Tea parties. Innocent child's play. A relaxing afternoon of make-believe,
or maybe special memories of time spent with a favorite aunt or loving
grandmother. Tea parties are reminders of simpler times, untroubled times.
But tea can even bring opposing sides together, if only for a moment of peace.
In October 1998, nearly three and a half years after China halted talks
with Taiwan, the two sides came together over tea, ending a period of
silence fraught with heightened anxiety and fear of war.
One year earlier, in October 1997, then First Lady Hillary Clinton was
visiting Belfast, Northern Ireland, when she implored leaders to do as the
women of Belfast do and work out their problems over "lots of tea."
This delightful coffee cake is a welcomed treat at any tea party.*

1. Preheat oven to 350° F.

2. In medium bowl, pour boiling water over tea bags; cover and brew
5 minutes. Remove tea bags.

3. Stir in apple and 2 tablespoons sugar until sugar is dissolved.

4. Let stand 1 hour. Remove apples; set aside. Reserve $^1/_4$ tea liquid.

5. In small bowl, combine flour, baking powder, and baking soda;
set aside.

6. In large mixer bowl, with electric mixer, beat butter and remaining
sugar until blended.

7. Beat in eggs, sour cream, reserved tea liquid, and vanilla.
Gradually beat in flour mixture until well blended. Stir in apples.

8. To make the apple crumb topping, combine sugar, flour, and
cinnamon in a small bowl.

9. With pastry blender or fingers, cut or rub in butter until mixture is the size of small peas.

10. Stir in walnuts or pecans.

11. Turn apple mixture into greased 9-inch springform pan. Top with apple crumb topping.

12. Bake uncovered for 1 hour or until toothpick inserted in center comes out clean. Let cool on wire rack before removing from pan.

TARTE AU SUCRE

Canadians are mad for tea, drinking over 7 billion cups a year.
This wonderfully rich pie is similar to the South's popular pecan pie,
but with a distinctly Canadian twist—combining maple syrup and tea.

1. Preheat oven to 450° F.

2. Chill the pie shell while preparing filling.

3. In a bowl, whisk together the eggs and sugar. Add the syrup, butter, tea, vinegar, and salt. Whisk until smooth. Stir in the nuts.

4. Place the pie shell on a cookie sheet, and pour the filling into the shell.

5. Bake in preheated oven for 10 minutes.

6. Lower the heat to 350° F and bake until the center is still a bit wiggly. It will set completely when cooled for about 25 minutes.

7. Cool and serve with sweetened whipped cream.

---

3 tablespoons cold butter, cut into pieces

1/2 cup chopped walnuts or pecans

YIELD: 9-INCH PIE

1 (9-inch) pie shell

3 eggs

3/4 cup plus 2 tablespoons light brown sugar

3/4 cup pure maple syrup

6 tablespoons unsalted butter, melted

1/4 cup brewed tea (Earl Grey is suggested)

2 tablespoons plus 1/2 teaspoon cider vinegar

Pinch salt

3/4 cup chopped walnuts, toasted

Whipped cream

WILD BLACK CURRANT BARS

YIELD: ABOUT 10 BARS

1 1/4 cups all purpose flour

1 1/4 cups powdered sugar

3/4 cup softened butter

1 package (8 ounces) cream cheese

1 cup granulated sugar

1 cup flaked coconut

2 eggs

1/2 teaspoon baking powder

1/4 teaspoon salt

12 Stash Tea Wild Blackcurrant tea bags

1 tablespoon water

Black currant tea, cream cheese, and coconut give these scrumptious bars a rich and tropical flavor.

1. Mix 1 cup flour with 1/4 cup powdered sugar and 1/2 cup butter until crumbly.

2. Pat into a greased 13-x-9-inch baking pan and bake at 375° F for 7–10 minutes, or until lightly browned.

3. To make the filling, combine cream cheese, granulated sugar, and coconut and blend well.

4. Beat in eggs, 2 tablespoons of flour, the baking powder, salt, contents of 10 tea bags, and 2 tablespoons melted butter until mixture is well blended.

5. Spread mixture over browned crust. Return to oven for 15–20 minutes, or until set.

6. To make the frosting, mix 1 cup powdered sugar, 1 tablespoon soft butter, 1 tablespoon water, and the contents of the 2 remaining tea bags until smooth.

7. Spread over the filled crust while still warm and let cool.

MAIN MEALS, SIDE SENSATIONS, AND SAUCES

APPLE CINNAMON GLAZED TURKEY

*Pair apple with cinnamon for a winning combination that turns
this tea-glazed turkey into a special dish your guests will love.*

1. Preheat oven to 325° F.

2. To create the apple cinnamon glaze, place the tea bags in a cup and add the boiling water. Let steep for 4 minutes and remove tea bags.

3. In a saucepan, combine the tea with corn syrup and brown sugar. Mix well.

4. Bring to a boil and let cool.

5. Place turkey, breast up, in a 12-x-17-inch roasting pan.

6. Baste turkey with 1 cup of the glaze.

7. Cook according to instructions on outer wrapper.

8. Halfway through cooking, glaze turkey once again.

9. Remove cooked turkey from oven, transfer to a serving platter and garnish.

YIELD: **8–10** SERVINGS

10 Stash Tea
Apple Cinnamon
tea bags

1 cup boiling water

2 cups corn syrup

2/3 cup brown sugar

1 turkey
(10–15 pounds)

CHAI SWEET SPICY SAUCE OVER CORNISH GAME HENS

YIELD: 2–4 SERVINGS

4 Stash Tea Chai Spice
tea bags

1/2 cup boiling water

I cup corn syrup

1/3 cup brown sugar

2–4 Cornish game
hens

1. Preheat over to 300° F.

2. Place the tea bags in a cup and add the boiling water. Let steep for 4 minutes. Remove tea bags.

3. Place corn syrup and brown sugar in a saucepan and add the tea concentrate. Mix well.

4. Bring sauce to a boil. Let cool.

5. Pour sauce over Cornish hens and bake for about 40 minutes to 1 hour. Baste hens 2–3 times as they cook.

CHAI SPICE STUFFING

YIELD: 4 SERVINGS

4 Stash Tea Chai Spice
tea bags

1/2 cup boiling water

I tablespoon olive oil

1/2 cup chopped celery

1/2 cup chopped green
onions

1/2 cup chopped
shallots

7 1/2 ounces
unseasoned bread
crumbs

2 eggs

1/2 teaspoon salt

1/2 teaspoon pepper

For a delicious added touch, try stuffing Cornish hens or other poultry with this spicy stuffing before baking them.

1. Preheat oven to 300° F.

2. Place the tea bags in a cup and add the boiling water. Allow to steep 5 minutes. Remove tea bags.

3. In a medium size saucepan, combine olive oil, celery, green onions, and shallots. Cook over medium heat until soft.

4. In a large bowl combine bread crumbs, sautéed vegetables, eggs, salt, pepper, and chai tea concentrate. Mix well.

5. Bake for approximately 30 minutes. Serve as a side dish or use as a poultry stuffing.

ROASTED CHAI CHICKEN

YIELD: 4 SERVINGS

1 chicken

Salt

½ onion

3 cloves garlic

1-inch slice fresh ginger root

2 tablespoons Oregon Chai Original Chai concentrate

1 tablespoon reduced sodium soy sauce

5 fresh figs, cut in half, lengthwise

*Surely everyone is aware of the divine pleasures which attend a wintry fireside;
candles at four o'clock, warm hearth rugs, tea, a fair tea-maker,
shutters closed, curtains flowing in ample draperies to the floor,
while the wind and rain are raging audibly without.*

—THOMAS DE QUINCEY (1785–1859)
ENGLISH AUTHOR

*Double the pleasure of a wintry fireside with this terrific
chai tea-seasoned recipe for roasted chicken.*

1. Preheat oven to 325° F.

2. Rinse chicken in cold water and drain.

3. Rub salt in cavity and place chicken in baking dish.

4. Stuff cavity with onion, garlic, ginger, chai concentrate, soy sauce, and fig halves, placing one fig half under the skin next to each breast.

5. Bake for 1 hour or until golden and the legs move easily.

6. Baste with juices every 15 minutes.

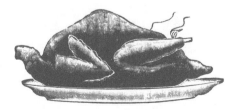

YIELD: **4 SERVINGS**

4 tablespoons orange
spice tea, prepared
strong

¾ cup peach or
apricot preserves

4 chicken breasts
(about 4 ounces each)

ORANGE SPICE CHICKEN

*Tea's proper use is to amuse the idle, and relax the studious, and dilute the
full meals of those who cannot use exercise, and will not use abstinence.*

—SAMUEL JOHNSON (1709–1784)
ENGLISH AUTHOR AND LEXICOGRAPHER

*Samuel Johnson was one of the most important literary figures of the
eighteenth century. He was nicknamed "Dictionary Johnson" for his
work compiling and writing the* Dictionary of the English Language
*in 1755. Despite his literary fame, he is probably best known for his
love of tea. He is often quoted today, well over 200 years after his death.*

*I am a hardened and shameless tea drinker, who has for twenty years diluted
his meals only with the infusion of this fascinating plant; whose kettle has
scarcely time to cool; who with tea amuses the evening, with tea solaces
the midnight, and with tea welcomes the morning.*

*Johnson's fondness for tea would be doubly appreciated
in this sweet sauce that's perfect for poultry.*

1. Preheat oven to 350° F.

2. Mix tea with preserves.

3. Brush mixture on chicken breasts.

4. Bake for 30–45 minutes, or until thoroughly cooked.

TEA SMOKED CHICKEN

*Black tea leaves, paired with poultry and citrus seasoning,
create a savory blend for this sensational smoky chicken dish.*

1. Line the lid and surface of a wok or stockpot with heavy-duty aluminum foil.

2. In a small bowl, mix together the tea leaves, brown sugar, orange and lemon peels, and rice. Spread mixture in the bottom of the wok.

3. Place a rack in the wok about three inches above the tea mixture. Place chicken on top of the rack.

4. Place wok over high heat. When mixture begins to smoke, cover with a lid. Lid should be tight-fitting to keep the smoke in.

5. Let smoke for 5 minutes, and then reduce heat to medium and continue cooking for 15 minutes.

6. Turn heat off and keep wok covered for another 15 minutes, or until the smoke subsides.

7. Remove cooked chicken from pan.

8. Lightly brush with sesame oil and serve.

YIELD: 4 SERVINGS

¹/₂ cup black tea leaves

¹/₂ cup brown sugar

1 tablespoon grated orange peel

1 tablespoon grated lemon peel

¹/₂ cup raw rice

4 chicken breasts, boneless and skinless

Sesame oil

YIELD: 4 (4-OUNCE) SERVINGS OR 2 (8-OUNCE) SERVINGS

I pound halibut steak or filet (or other white fish)

4 tablespoons milk

4 tablespoons cooking sherry (or white wine)

Salt to taste

Pepper to taste

Garlic powder to taste

2 Stash Tea Lemon Blossom tea bags

1/4 cup sliced mushrooms

1/4 cup sliced onions

LEMON HERB HALIBUT

Build variety into your recipes with herbal teas. This simple seafood dish is an excellent example of how herbal teas can be used to season food. The wonderful combinations of herbs found in herbal teas can add unique flavors to meats, seafood, and even salads and sauces.

1. Preheat oven to 325° F.

2. Spray baking dish with nonstick cooking spray. Place halibut in the dish.

3. Add milk and cooking sherry. Sprinkle with salt, pepper, garlic powder, and the contents of 1 tea bag.

4. Place mushroom and onion slices on top of fish.

5. Sprinkle with more salt, pepper, garlic powder, and contents of the remaining tea bag.

6. Place lid over mixture and cook for approximately 25 minutes. Check fish after 20 minutes, making sure not to overcook.

LEMON AND DILL SALMON

YIELD: 2 CUPS

1 ¾ cups salmon, skinned and boned

⅔ cup butter, softened

2 Stash Tea Lemon Blossom tea bags

1 tablespoon water

2 teaspoons chopped fresh dill

Salt and pepper to taste

If you were the Queen of England, how would you commemorate a marital milestone? With a tea party, of course. Queen Elizabeth II and her husband, Prince Philip, celebrated their fiftieth wedding anniversary by inviting 4,000 couples to Buckingham Palace for tea. Only couples who were married the same year as the royal pair were invited, and those who got married on the same day, November 20, 1947, were treated to a private party with the Queen and Prince, where, no doubt, many a teacup was raised to praise their golden celebration.

1. Flake the salmon into a bowl together with butter, contents of tea bags, water, and dill.

2. Blend with a mixer or food processor until very smooth.

3. Spoon mixture into small bowl and serve on a platter surrounded by bread sticks and/or raw vegetables.

TERRIFIC TEA MARINADE

YIELD: 1½ CUPS

1 cup black tea, prepared strong

2 tablespoons sesame oil

½ cup soy sauce

¼ tablespoon garlic powder

Food can also benefit from a good marinade. This tea-riffic marinade adds a wonderfully smoky flavor to most fish and poultry. Be sure to use it with grilled salmon or baked chicken.

1. In a bowl, combine cooled tea with the sesame oil, soy sauce, and garlic powder. Mix well.

2. Use the mixture to marinate up to 1 pound of fish or poultry.

I package (15–16 ounces) Chinese-style firm or extra firm tofu, pressed

3 teaspoons extra virgin olive oil

¼ cup chopped onion

I cup white Basmati rice

2 teaspoons curry powder, or to taste

I cup brewed black tea

I cup water

2 tablespoons tamari soy sauce

I vegetable bouillon cube or I teaspoon dry vegetable bouillon or broth

2 tablespoons white wine vinegar

I teaspoon sugar or other sweetener

I cup diced celery

I cup bell pepper, diced (preferably use two or more colors)

CURRIED RICE SALAD

This flavorful rice dish demonstrates the versatility of cooking with tea. Experiment by using brewed tea like a broth for rice, pasta dishes, and soups, for example. The possibilities are limited only by your imagination.

1. Cut the tofu into half-inch slices.

2. Heat 1 teaspoon of the oil in a heavy skillet over medium heat. Add the tofu and brown on one side, then turn and brown the other side. Drain on a paper towel and let cool. Cut into half-inch cubes; set aside.

3. In the same skillet heat the remaining 2 teaspoons of oil over medium heat. Add the onion and sauté for 2 or 3 minutes. Add the rice and curry powder and continue to sauté until the onions are tender but not browned.

4. Stir in the tea, water, tamari, and bouillon. Raise heat and bring to a boil (if using a bouillon cube, break it up with a spatula until completely dissolved).

5. Reduce heat to low and simmer, covered, until all liquid is absorbed, about 15 or 20 minutes.

6. Meanwhile, in a small bowl, mix together the vinegar and sugar until sugar is dissolved.

7. When the rice is fully cooked, remove the skillet from the heat and stir in the vinegar mixture along with the tofu and celery, bell pepper, and scallion. Toss with a fork and spoon until all ingredients are well mixed.

8. Adjust seasonings if necessary. Transfer to a serving dish or storage container and cool to room temperature or chill in the refrigerator. Serve cool or chilled.

1 scallion, white and green parts, thinly sliced

Salt and pepper to taste (optional)

WILD RASPBERRY VINAIGRETTE

This refreshing vinaigrette is a great salad topper. It also lends a flavorful spark to pasta and vegetable dishes.

1. In a jar, combine contents of Wild Raspberry tea bags, balsamic vinegar, water, and olive oil. Shake well.

2. Refrigerate and serve.

YIELD: 1½ CUPS

8 Stash Tea Wild Raspberry tea bags

1 cup balsamic vinegar

¼ cup water

¼ cup virgin olive oil

½ cup strong lapsang
souchong or other
black tea

I tablespoon oyster
sauce

I tablespoon fish sauce

I tablespoon mirin

I tablespoon tamari
(or light soy sauce)

I tablespoon toasted
sesame oil

I teaspoon brown
sugar

I clove garlic, minced

2 tablespoons
vegetable oil

½ teaspoon hot
pepper flakes

I small onion, halved
and sliced

½ red pepper, chopped

½ yellow pepper,
chopped

I cup sliced snow peas

2 cups cooked basmati
rice

2 green onions,
chopped

FRIED TEA-SCENTED BASMATI RICE

*For a fast, one-dish meal, add stir-fried chicken tenders,
shrimp, or scallops to this flavorful rice.*

1. In bowl, whisk together the tea, oyster sauce, fish sauce, mirin, tamari, sesame oil, brown sugar, and garlic; set aside.

2. Heat the vegetable oil in wok or deep skillet set over medium-high heat; add hot pepper flakes and cook 1 minute until fragrant.

3. Add the onion and stir-fry for 5 minutes, or until it softens and starts to become brown.

4. Increase heat to high and add the red and yellow peppers; cook, stirring occasionally, for 3 minutes or until beginning to brown.

5. Add snow peas and reserved tea mixture; boil for 2 minutes or until liquid is reduced and syrupy.

6. Add rice and green onions. Cook, while tossing, for 3 minutes or until heated through.

PASTA SALAD WITH EARL GREY TEA VINAIGRETTE

YIELD: 4–6 SERVINGS

What do caviar and creamed chicken, mousse of foie gras and lamb stew, champagne and Earl Grey tea have in common? All were served on the buffet table at the wedding party of the twentieth century's most controversial marriage. Some might think the food pairings were as unusual as the couple themselves.

In 1936, England's King Edward VIII gave up his crown to marry the twice-divorced American "commoner" Wallis Warfield Simpson. Many thought it was foolish, many more thought it was hopelessly romantic. What is certain is that the union of the Duke and Duchess of Windsor became the love story of the century. After the ceremony, with the exception of a champagne toast to his new bride, the Duke drank only Earl Grey tea.

Earl Grey dresses this pasta salad into a fitting recipe for any fine event.

4 cups cooked fusilli or other pasta

1 cup diced red pepper

1 cup diced green pepper

1 cup finely chopped red onion

Vinaigrette

½ cup Earl Grey tea, prepared strong

2 tablespoons orange juice

½ teaspoon granulated sugar

1 tablespoon rice wine vinegar

1 tablespoon minced shallots

1 clove garlic, minced

¼ teaspoon salt

¼ teaspoon pepper

2 tablespoons sesame oil

¼ cup chopped fresh basil

1. To prepare the vinaigrette, place the tea, orange juice, and sugar in a small pan or skillet and bring to a boil; cook until reduced to about 2 tablespoons.

2. Add the vinegar, shallots, garlic, salt, pepper, and sesame oil to the tea mixture. Stir in the basil and set aside. (This dressing, which doubles easily, can be made up to two days ahead.)

3. In a large bowl, toss together the pasta, peppers, and onion. Drizzle with vinaigrette and toss to combine. Taste and adjust seasoning, if desired.

HOT AND SOUR SESAME NOODLES

12 ounces linguine,
fettuccine,
or eggless noodles

I teaspoon sunflower,
peanut, or other
light oil

¼ cup tomato paste

¼ cup rice, apple cider,
or balsamic vinegar

⅓ cup tea, regular
strength

2 tablespoons maple
syrup, rice syrup, or
other liquid sweetener

I tablespoon tamari
soy sauce

I teaspoon garlic
powder, or 2 large
cloves roasted garlic,
minced

½ teaspoon crushed
cayenne pepper flakes

I teaspoon gomasio
(sesame salt)

I teaspoon sesame oil

Better to be deprived of food for three days, than tea for one.

—ANCIENT CHINESE PROVERB

1. Prepare the noodles to al dente tenderness. Drain and either return to the pot (if serving this dish hot) or rinse with cold water and place in large bowl (if serving cold).

2. Toss the cooked pasta with the oil; set aside.

3. Mix the tomato paste and vinegar together in a small bowl. Add the remaining ingredients and mix well.

4. Spoon the sauce over the pasta and mix well to coat.

5. Sprinkle with additional gomasio before serving.

VARIATION

Add any or all of the following ingredients to the cooked noodles before mixing with the sauce:

½ pound tofu (Chinese style, extra-firm or well-pressed firm), cut into half-inch cubes

I cup fresh mung bean sprouts

I cup lightly cooked chopped broccoli

½ cup slivered canned water chestnuts

½ cup slivered raw or lightly cooked snow peas

If you don't want to add additional salt, sprinkle the noodles with plain toasted sesame seeds (whole or crushed) in place of the gomasio, or garnish with thinly sliced scallions.

HOMESTYLE GINGERED TOFU

Thank God for tea! What would the world do without tea!
How did it exist? I am glad I was not born before tea.

—SYDNEY SMITH (1771–1845), ENGLISH CLERGYMAN AND AUTHOR

While Mr. Smith took delight in drinking tea, he might be surprised by the many ways tea is used today. Tea is coming of age in today's kitchens, and virtually nothing is considered taboo. This flavorful recipe will satisfy both the hungry and the health conscious.

1. Pour the tea into a medium saucepan and bring to a light boil.

2. Add the tofu and boil for 10 minutes over medium heat.

3. Remove the tofu to a plate or bowl with slotted spoon.

4. Leave only 2 cups of the tea in the saucepan (you can water your plants with the remaining tea when it cools).

5. Add the ginger and soy sauce to saucepan, stir, and bring to a boil.

6. Mix the arrowroot with the water until smooth. Pour it slowly into the saucepan, while stirring. Continue to stir until the sauce thickens.

7. Lower the heat to simmer, and add the peanuts and scallions. Cook, while stirring, for another minute.

8. Remove from heat and carefully add the tofu, stirring gently. Serve over cooked rice or pasta.

VARIATION

In place of peanuts, try slivered toasted almonds. Or try slivered water chestnuts for the same crunch and less fat (but less protein).

---

3 cups tea
(your choice)
regular strength

I pound extra firm
or pressed firm tofu,
cut into 1-inch cubes

2 teaspoons grated
or finely chopped
fresh ginger

1/4 cup tamari soy
sauce, regular or
low-sodium

1/4 cup arrowroot
powder or cornstarch

1/2 cup water or tea
(room temperature
or cooler)

1/4 cup roasted,
unsalted peanuts

3–4 scallions, green
part only, shredded

About 3 cups cooked
brown or basmati rice,
or cooked pasta

TEA THYME SOUP

YIELD: 4–6 SERVINGS

5 cups vegetable stock, broth, or bouillon

4 large cloves garlic, minced or pressed

3 teaspoons lightly crushed dried thyme

3 cups chopped broccoli, fresh or frozen

8 ounces macaroni (small shells, wagon wheels, fusilli, or other shape)

I cup green tea, regular strength

Juice of I lemon (about 2 tablespoons)

$1/8$ teaspoon freshly ground black pepper, or to taste

Salt to taste (optional)

If you are cold, tea will warm you;
If your are too heated, it will cool you;
If you are depressed, it will cheer you;
If you are excited; it will calm you.

—WILLIAM EWART GLADSTONE (1809–1898)
BRITISH STATESMAN AND PRIME MINISTER

The blessings of tea are counted by many.
The ways to enjoy tea are limited only by your imagination.
This savory soup recipe is an excellent example.

1. Combine the stock, garlic, and thyme in a heavy saucepan and bring to a boil.

2. Stir in the broccoli and macaroni, reduce the heat, and simmer 8–12 minutes, or until the macaroni is just al dente.

3. Stir in the tea and heat for 1 minute.

4. Remove from the heat and stir in the lemon juice, pepper, and salt, if desired. Serve piping hot.

VARIATIONS

Substitute other chopped cruciferous vegetables (cabbage, cauliflower, Brussels sprouts, kohlrabi) for all or part of the broccoli.

For a main-dish soup, add $1/2$ pound firm tofu (diced), or 1 cup cooked or canned beans (rinsed and well drained) to the pot along with the green tea.

Conclusion

Y ou've come to the end of *Tales of a Tea Leaf,* but it's really just the beginning. New tales of tea are being written every day. New tea companies are constantly forming, blends are being created, and new health benefits are being discovered. As the world's most beloved beverage, tea has tremendous staying power. With nearly 5,000 years of history behind it, tea's popularity shows no signs of slowing down. In fact, modern-day marketers are attempting to turn this ancient elixir into the next "new" drink. And as we've seen, American tea companies have done a good job of reinventing tea's image. But despite all the recent media attention, the charms of tea remain unchanged. Hot or cold, sipped alone or with friends, tea comforts and cheers us. The simple satisfaction found in a cup of tea is a universal pleasure enjoyed as much today as in ancient times.

I hope you've enjoyed these tea tales. Maybe you've learned something new, or have been inspired to seek out your local tea shop and try a new kind of tea, or even host your own tea-tasting party. Would you like to learn more about this fascinating beverage? This book's Resource List is a great place to start. You'll find tea organizations and companies, tea publications, and even tea events you can attend! There is a wealth of additional information on everything tea, so this list is a perfect place to begin your own tale of tea. I hope you enjoy the journey as much as I have.

Metric Conversion Tables

COMMON LIQUID CONVERSIONS

Measurement	=	Milliliters
$1/4$ teaspoon	=	1.25 milliliters
$1/2$ teaspoon	=	2.50 milliliters
$3/4$ teaspoon	=	3.75 milliliters
1 teaspoon	=	5.00 milliliters
$1 1/4$ teaspoons	=	6.25 milliliters
$1 1/2$ teaspoons	=	7.50 milliliters
$1 3/4$ teaspoons	=	8.75 milliliters
2 teaspoons	=	10.0 milliliters
1 tablespoon	=	15.0 milliliters
2 tablespoons	=	30.0 milliliters

Measurement	=	Liters
$1/4$ cup	=	0.06 liters
$1/2$ cup	=	0.12 liters
$3/4$ cup	=	0.18 liters
1 cup	=	0.24 liters
$1 1/4$ cups	=	0.30 liters
$1 1/2$ cups	=	0.36 liters
2 cups	=	0.48 liters
$2 1/2$ cups	=	0.60 liters
3 cups	=	0.72 liters
$3 1/2$ cups	=	0.84 liters
4 cups	=	0.96 liters
$4 1/2$ cups	=	1.08 liters
5 cups	=	1.20 liters
$5 1/2$ cups	=	1.32 liters

CONVERSION FORMULAS

LIQUID

When You Know	Multiply By	To Determine
teaspoons	5.0	milliliters
tablespoons	15.0	milliliters
fluid ounces	30.0	milliliters
cups	0.24	liters
pints	0.47	liters
quarts	0.95	liters

WEIGHT

When You Know	Multiply By	To Determine
ounces	28.0	grams
pounds	0.45	kilograms

CONVERTING FAHRENHEIT TO CELSIUS

Fahrenheit	=	Celsius
200–205	=	95
220–225	=	105
245–250	=	120
275	=	135
300–305	=	150
325–330	=	165
345–350	=	175
370–375	=	190
400–405	=	205
425–430	=	220
445–450	=	230
470–475	=	245
500	=	260

ResourceList

The following section contains essential information for you as you further explore the many tales of the tea leaf. Use these organizations, publications, and websites as an excellent starting point for your voyage. If you are interested in purchasing tea and tea accessories—or anything related to tea—check out the companies listed below, too. Each company's website contains a comprehensive online store, making it easier than ever for you to savor the gourmet brews and exotic blends that may not have yet found their way to your local supermarket. So, make yourself your favorite tea and get started!

TEA ASSOCIATIONS & ORGANIZATIONS

**Australian Food and
Grocery Council
Tea Industry Forum**
Website: *www.tea.org.au*

The Darjeeling Tea Network
Website: *www.darjeelingtea.com*

Herb Research Foundation
4140 15th Street
Boulder, CO 80304
Phone: (303) 449-2265 · (800) 748-2617
Website: *www.herbs.org*

International Tea Committee
Website: *www.inttea.com*

**Miss Ponchick's Tea Tag Project
(See also Teaneck Tea)**
c/o Whittier School
491 West Englewood Avenue
Teaneck, NJ 07666
Phone: (201) 833-5535

The Red Hat Society
431 South Acacia Avenue
Fullerton, CA 92831
Phone: (714) 738-0001
Website: *www.redhatsociety.com*

A national "disorganization" of women over fifty who get together—wearing their red hats and gloves—to drink tea, share stories, and socialize.

Sage Group International, LLC
PO Box 9969
Seattle, WA 98109
Website: www.teareport.com

As creators of the highly respected Tea Is "Hot" Report, this specialty tea industry research group provides a resource of information on statistics, trends, products, and scientific research relating to tea and the business of tea.

Specialty Tea Institute/Tea Association of the USA/Tea Council
420 Lexington Avenue
New York, NY 10170
Phone: (212) 986-9415
Website: *www.teausa.com*

The Specialty Tea Institute is a new organization merging the American Premium Tea Institute and the Specialty Tea Registry.

Sri Lanka Tea Board
PO Box 1750
Colombo
Sri Lanka
Website: *www.pureceylontea.com*

The Tea Association (TTA)
Website: *www.stud.ntnu.no/~havarwi/ teklubb/english*

An independent organization dedicating to sharing information on the joys of tea. The Tea Association was started in Norway by a group of young men in their 20s.

Tea Association of Canada
Website: *www.tea.ca*

**Tea Association of the USA
Tea Council of the USA**
420 Lexington Avenue
New York, NY
Phone: (212) 986-9415
Website: *www.teausa.com*

Tea Board of India
350 Fifth Avenue, #1124
New York, NY 10118
Phone: (212) 563-5261
Website: *www.teaindia.com*

The Tea Board of Kenya
Website: *www.teaboard.or.ke*

Tea Council of the UK
Website: *www.teacouncil.co.uk*

Tea Market Report/Van Rees Group
Website: *www.vanrees.com*

Tea Society
1629 Date Street
Montebello, CA 90640
Phone: (877) TEA-LAND
Website: *www.teasociety.org*

Tea Sourcing Partnership
Website: *www.teasourcingpartnership.org.uk*

Teaneck Tea
Phone: (888) 427-6398
Website: *www.harney.com*

Urasenke Foundation
Websites:
    www.urasenke.or.jp/texte/index.html
    San Francisco: *www.urasenke.org*
    Seattle: *www.urasenkeseattle.org*
    Washington, DC: *www.urasenkedc.org*
Extensive information on the Japanese tea ceremony.

World Green Tea Organization
Website: *www.o-cha.net*

An organization dedicated to spreading information on the culture, health benefits, and business of tea. The goal is to increase awareness of the beneficial functions of green tea.

TEA COMPANIES

Affinitea Brewing Technologies, Inc.
PMB 323
6523 California Avenue SW
Seattle, WA 98136
Phone: (800) 891-6785
Website: *www.affinitea.com*

Makers of the Affinitea Beverage Infuser, a piece of equipment similar to an espresso machine that provides high-quality tea beverages (hot or iced) in about thirty seconds. Affinitea also offers a selection of superb beverages specially blended for use with the Infuser, including loose leaf teas, herbs, and fruit juices.

Albert Uster Imports
Phone: (800) 231-8154
Website: *www.auiswisscatalogue.com*

Importers of such fine gourmet products as Läderach Dark Chocolate Soufflé Cups.

American Classic Tea
Charleston Tea Gardens
6617 Maybank Highway
Wadmalaw Island, SC 29487
Phone: (800) 443-5987
Website: *www.bigelowtea.com*

Charleston Tea Gardens, "America's only tea garden," grows and produces a black tea that is known as American Classic Tea. This tea is said to be directly descended from ancestral tea bushes that were brought into the United States from China and India a century ago.

R.C. Bigelow
201 Black Rock Turnpike
Fairfield, CT 06825
Phone: (888) BIGELOW
Website: *www.bigelowtea.com*

*Website offers a variety of teas, gift sets, teapots, tea
accessories, and more.*

Carnelian Rose Tea Company
1803 Main Street
Vancouver, WA 98660
Phone: (360) 573-0917
Website: *www.carnelianrosetea.com*

*Offers a wide variety of teas—black, green, oolong,
herbal, white, rooibos, and others—as well as various
tea-related gifts and accessories.*

**Celestial Seasonings
(Hain Celestial Group)**
4600 Sleepytime Drive
Boulder, CO 80301
Phone: (303) 581-1202
Website: *www.celestialseasonings.com*

*Offers a wide range of teas and tea products, plus
health news and resources on everything about
herbs and tea.*

Fortnum & Mason
Website: *www.fortnumandmason.com*

*The online store for this 300-year-old London
establishment is where you can order an exclusive
range of fine teas and other gourmet products.*

Good Earth Tea
PO Box 1606
Nokomis, FL 34274
Phone: (941) 412-3799
Website: *www.goodearth.com*

*Provides a wide selection of teas, as well as tea
information, health news, and recipes.*

Harney & Sons Fine Teas
PO Box 665
Salisbury, CT 06068
Phone: (888) HARNEYT or (888) 427-6398
Website: *www.harney.com*

*Offers unique array of tea, exclusive tea blends, art teas,
gifts, accessories, and tea trivia.*

Honest Tea
5019 Wilson Lane
Bethesda, MD 20814
Phone: (800) 865-4736
Website: *www.honesttea.com*

*Tea the way nature intended it to be—freshly brewed with
select tea leaves and minimally sweetened. Honest Tea is
committed to providing healthy, organic beverages while
maintaining social responsibility.*

Indonesian Tea—Sosro
Website: *www.sosro.com*

*Provides information on Sosro, an Indonesian brand
of ready-to-drink flavored tea beverages and tea bags.
The website also offers information on the history,
processing, and types of tea.*

Kombucha Wonder Drink
1235 SW 16th Avenue
Portland, OR 97205
Phone: (877) 224-7331
Website: *www.wonderdrink.com*

Offers information on Kombucha Wonder Drink, a traditional Asian beverage fermented from the Kombucha culture, which contains minimal amounts of caffeine and calories. There have been many reports praising this drink for its various health benefits.

Lipton Tea
800 Sylvan Avenue
Englewood Cliffs, NJ 07632
Phone: (888) LIPTONT
Website: *www.lipton.com*

Provides extensive information on Lipton tea products, as well as research findings on tea and health, and antioxidants. Also offers a variety of tea recipes, and interesting tea trivia.

Numi Teas and Teasans
PO Box 20420
Oakland, CA 94620
Phone: (888) 404-6864
Website: *www.numitea.com*

In addition to Numi's selection of real tea and herbal teas, its online store offers tea accessories, flowering teas, bamboo boxes and gift sets, and more. Numi uses organic tea, and is dedicated to sustainability, fair trade, and social responsibility. Also provides extensive information on tea and your health and explains the various types of teas of the world.

Oregon Chai
1745 NW Marshall Street
Portland, OR 97209
Phone: (888) 874-CHAI
Website: *www.oregonchai.com*

A producer of a variety of chai tea latte concentrates and mixes, Oregon Chai uses organic, natural ingredients in its products, which include hot and iced drinks. Website contains product information as well as many recipes.

Red Rose
Website: *www.redrosetea.com*

Red Rose produces tea blends made from tea leaves grown at higher elevations on mountain tea estates—leading to a higher quality tea. It offers information on the history of tea, Red Rose tea products, and recipes.

Serendipitea
3229 Greenpoint Avenue
Long Island City, NY 11101
Phone: (888) TEA-LIFE
Website: *www.serendipitea.com*

Offers numerous tea varieties including tisanes, Yixing and other teapots, accessories, and gifts. The website also provides a guide to the origins and rituals associated with tea, as well as information on the many types of tea.

Sir Aubrey's Tea Company, Ltd.
White Lion Traditional Tea
8260 E. Gelding, #103
Scottsdale, AZ 85260
Phone: (480) 607-5300
Website: *www.siraubrey.com*

Sir Aubrey's Tea Company and White Lion Traditional Tea offer an array of gourmet premium teas.

Stash Tea
PO Box 910
Portland, OR 97207
Phone: (800) 800-TEAS
Website: *www.stashtea.com*

Has an extensive catalog of teas, teapots, gifts and other tea-related items. In addition to its online store, Stash's website presents facts on tea and offers recipes.

Steep Tea
Phone: (800) STEEP-CO
Website: *www.steep.com*

An innovative tea company that is very youth-oriented.

Tata Tea
Website: *www.tatatea.com*

The parent of The Tetley Group, along with several other tea brands, this India-based company is dedicated to social and community development.

Tazo Tea
PO Box 66
Portland, OR 97207
Phone: (800) 299-9445
Website: *www.tazo.com*

Tazo Tea produces a variety of original tea blends, including loose leaf tea, concentrates, and lattes.

Tetley Tea
Phone: (800) 728-0084
Website: *www.tetley.com*

Website offers information on tea and health, tea recipes, the Tea Shoppe (an online catalog featuring a selection of teas), and more.

The Republic of Tea
8 Digital Drive, Suite 100
Novato, CA 94949
Phone: (800) 298-4832
Website: *www.republicoftea.com*

This unique tea company is described as the "leading purveyor of premium teas" and offers a wide selection of teas, as well as tea facts and information on brewing tea.

R. Twining & Co., Ltd.
Website: *www.twinings.com*

Explores the history and tradition of tea and offers an array of teas. Also offers a unique "tea finder" based upon your preferences for strength and flavor.

Williamson Magor Group
Website: *www.wmtea.com*

This company is one of the foremost producers of Assam quality teas. Williamson Magor Group is based in India and has twenty-eight tea estates throughout Southeast Asia.

Williamson Tea Assam Ltd.
Website: *www.williamsonteaassam.com*

Founded in 1869, this company is still family owned and operated. Williamson Tea Assam has seventeen tea estates in Assam, India.

Yogi Tea
2545 Prairie Road
Eugene, OR 97402
Phone: (800) YOGI-TEA
Website: *www.yogitea.com*

In addition to an array of teas that includes many healing formulas, this company's website provides an extensive herb glossary. Its clever "find-your-tea" section, helps you choose the best formula to suit your needs.

BOOKS

Lu Yu, *The Classic of Tea*. Translator: Francis Ross Carpenter. Little, Brown and Company, New York; 1974.

Okakura, Kakuzo, *The Book of Tea*. Fox, Duffield and Company; 1906. Dover Publications, Inc., New York; 1964.

Perry, Sara, *The Tea Book: A Guide to Black, Green, Herbal and Chai Teas*. Chronicle Books, San Francisco; 2001.

Pratt, James Norwood, *New Tea Lover's Treasury*. Tea Society, San Francisco; 1999.

Pugh, Peter. *Williamson Magor Stuck To Tea*. Cambridge Business Publishing, Great Britain; 1991.

Resnick, Jane, *Loving Tea*. Berkley Books, New York; 1997.

Rubin, Ron and Stuart Avery Gold. *Tea Chings: The Tea and Herb Companion*. Newmarket Press, New York; 2002.

Schapira, Joel, David, and Karl. *The Book of Coffee & Tea: A Guide to the Appreciation of Fine Coffees, Teas, and Herbal Beverages*. St. Martin's Press, New York; 1975, 1982.

Wild, Antony. *The East India Company Book of Tea*. HarperCollins Publishers, London; 1994, 1995, 1997.

WEBSITES

The following websites are definitely worth a look for tea lovers—or for those interested in learning more about tea, including the tea varieties discussed in this book.

African Tea
www.africantea.com

British Teas & Products
www.EnglishTeaStore.com
www.britishdelights.com

Bubble Tea
www.bubbletea.com

Cat-Tea Corner
www.catteacorner.com

Dr. Andrew Weil
www.drweil.com

FML Tea Trading Co., Ltd.
www.fmltea.com

Holy Mountain Trading Company
www.holymtn.com

Kava
www.kavaroot.com

Kombucha
www.kombuchaamerica.com

Planet Tea
www.planet-tea.com

Sally's Place
www.sallys-place.com

TeaMuse
www.teamuse.com

Tea Time Worldwide
www.teatimeworldwide.com

Teas Etc.
www.teasetc.com

Yerba Mate
www.yerbamate.com

PUBLICATIONS

Fresh Cup Magazine
PO Box 14827
Portland, OR 97293-0827
Phone: (800) 868-5866
Website: *www.freshcup.com*

Tea A Magazine
3 Devotion Road
Scotland, CT 06264
Phone: (888) 456-8651
Website: *www.teamag.com*

Tea & Coffee Trade Journal
Phone: (212) 391-2060
Website: *www.teaandcoffee.net*

Tea and Roses Newsletter
51 Davenport Avenue
Morris Plains, NJ 07950
Phone: (973) 984-6081
Website: *www.tea-and-roses.com*

The Tea House Times
PO Box 1049
Sparta, NJ 07871
Website: *www.theteahousetimes.com*

TeaTime Gazette
Website: *www.teatimegazette.com*

TEA EVENTS

Canadian Coffee & Tea Expo
Phone: (416) 784-5210
Website: *www.coffee-expo.com*

NASCORE
(North American Specialty Coffee
& Beverage Retailers' Expo)
Specialty Coffee and Tea Tradeshow
Phone: (800) 548-0551
Website: *www.nascore.net*

Specialty Tea Institute Symposium
Phone: (212) 986-9415
Website: *www.teausa.com*

Tea Association of the USA
Annual Convention
Phone: (212) 986-9415
Website: *www.teausa.com*

Tea and Coffee World Cup
Phone: (212) 391-2060
Website: *www.tcworldcup.com*

World Tea Expo
Phone: (702) 253-1893
Website: *www.worldteaexpo.com*

World Tea Forum
Phone: (212) 986-9415
Website: *www.teausa.com*

Permission Credits

This book would not be possible without the generous contributions of the individuals and organizations listed below who have given permission to reprint, or have been a source for the recipes in this book. My sincere appreciation and thanks go out to all.

Bar-None Drink Recipes
www.barnonedrinks.com
Artillery Punch, 118
Boston Tea Hardy, 122
Ice Pick Tea, 116
Smooth Tickle Tea, 123

The Cat-Tea Corner
www.catteacorner.com
Recipes courtesy of Janis P. Badarau and The Cat-Tea Corner. Copyright © 1997–2005. Reprinted by permission.

Curried Rice Salad, 158–159
Homestyle Gingered Tofu, 163
Hot & Sour Sesame Noodles, 162
Tea Thyme Soup, 164

Celestial Seasonings, Inc.
www.celestialseasonsings.com
Nutcracker Sweet Pie, 145
    Celestial Seasonings, Inc. © 1996
Pumpkin Chai Pie, 138
    Celestial Seasonings, Inc. © 1998

Dream Ship: Coffees, Teas & Treasures
Apricot Tea Bread, 141
Dream Ship's Thai Iced Tea, 114

Emergent Media, Inc.
www.cookierecipe.com
www.pierecipe.com
Austrian Peach Cookies, 144–145
Tarte au Sucre, 149

Index

FOR THE LOVE OF GARLIC
The Complete Guide to Garlic Cuisine
Victoria Renoux

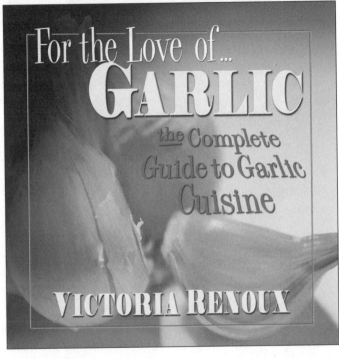

For the Love of Garlic is a celebration of an astonishingly versatile food. It explores garlic's past and present, and provides a wide variety of delicious kitchen-tested garlic recipes designed to tempt not only garlic aficionados, but all lovers of great cuisine.

Part One begins by looking at the history, lore, and many uses of this culinary treasure. It examines how garlic's active compounds have been proven to heal illness and maintain radiant health. Also included is a section on growing and buying this gourmet marvel. Part Two indulges in the tastes and pleasures of garlic. The author first discusses cooking techniques and special utensils that can enhance the use of this ingredient. She then offers eighty-five tempting dishes that will allow you to indulge all your garlic fantasies.

Whether given as a gift or used as a personal reference, this beautifully designed and illustrated work will prove itself to be a useful and informative guide time and time again.

$13.95 • 204 pages • 7.5 x 7.5-inch quality paperback • ISBN 0-7570-0087-8

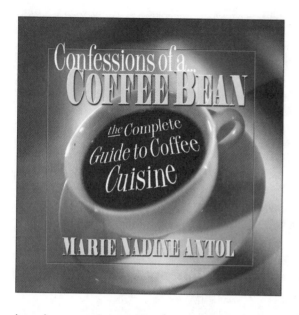

CONFESSIONS OF A COFFEE BEAN
The Complete Guide to Coffee Cuisine
Marie Nadine Antol

Yes, I have a few things to confess. But before I start, I just want you to know that I couldn't help it. It just happened. Everywhere I went, they wanted me. Now, I have a few things to share— I think it's time to spill the beans.

With a distinct aroma and an irresistible flavor, it has commanded the attention of the world. It is the coffee bean, and while many seek its pleasures, few know its secrets—the secrets of its origin and its appeal, and the key to getting the best out of the bean. Designed for lovers of coffee everywhere, here is a complete guide to understanding and enjoying this celebrated object of our affection.

Part One of Confessions of a Coffee Bean opens with the history of coffee and details the coffee bean's epic journey from crop to cup. It then describes the intriguing evolution of the coffeehouse, highlights surprising facts about coffee and your health, and provides an introduction to the most enticing coffees available today. Finally, this section presents everything you need to know about making a great cup of coffee, from selecting the beans to brewing a perfect pot.

Part Two is a tempting collection of recipes for both coffee drinks and coffee accompaniments. First, you'll learn to make a wide variety of coffee beverages, from steaming brews like Café au Lait to icy concoctions like the Espresso Shake. Then, you'll enjoy a bevy of desserts and other coffee companions, from classic crumb-topped cakes to coffee-kissed creations such as Rich Coffee Tiramisu. You'll even find recipes for coffee-laced candies and sauces.

Whether you're a true coffee aficionado or just someone who loves a good cup of java, this is a book that will entrance you with fascinating facts about all things coffee.

$13.95 • 204 pages • 7.5 x 7.5-inch quality paperback • ISBN 0-7570-0020-7

TOMMY TANG'S MODERN THAI CUISINE
Tommy Tang

Tommy Tang, celebrated chef and owner of Tommy Tang's restaurants in Los Angeles and New York, shares his flair for creating unique, delectable cuisine from his native Thailand. In *Tommy Tang's Modern Thai Cuisine*, Tommy presents over ninety of his signature recipes, which combine elements of Japanese, Indian, American, and European dishes with traditional Thai flavor. Enjoy delicacies like Thai Egg Rolls, Red Curry Shrimp, Soft Shell Crabs with Ginger-Garlic Sauce, Lemon Grass Chicken, and Tommy's special sushi. Easy-to-follow instructional illustrations guarantee professional results, while beautiful full-color photographs help you choose the perfect recipe for your next cooking adventure.

If you love Thai food, but have always thought that it was beyond your culinary reach, Tommy Tang is here to change your mind. Let *Tommy Tang's Modern Thai Cuisine* bring the joy of Thai cooking to your home.

$16.95 • 172 pages • 7.5 x 9-inch quality paperback • ISBN 0-7570-0254-4

THE SOPHISTICATED OLIVE
The Complete Guide to Olive Cuisine
Marie Nadine Antol

Simple, elegant, refined. With a history as old as the Bible, the humble olive has matured into a sophisticated culinary treasure. Enter any fine restaurant and you will find the sumptuous flavor of olives in cocktails, appetizers, salads, and entrées. Now, food writer Marie Nadine Antol has created *The Sophisticated Olive*, an informative guide to this glorious fruit's many healthful benefits, surprising uses, and spectacular tastes.

Part One begins by exploring the history of the olive and its range of remarkable properties, including its use as a beauty enhancer and health provider. It then goes on to describe the many olive varieties that are found throughout the world. Part Two presents over 100 kitchen-tested recipes, including salads, dressings, spreads, soups, side dishes, entrées, breads, and beverages—all designed to put a smile on the face of any olive lover.

$13.95 • 204 pages • 7.5 x 7.5-inch quality paperback • ISBN 0-7570-0024-X

GOING WILD IN THE KITCHEN
The Fresh & Sassy Tastes of Vegetarian Cooking
Leslie Cerier

Going Wild in the Kitchen is the first comprehensive global vegetarian cookbook to go beyond the standard organic beans, grains, and vegetables. In addition to providing helpful cooking tips and techniques, the book contains over 150 kitchen-tested recipes for healthful, taste-tempting dishes—creative masterpieces that contain such unique ingredients as edible flowers; sea vegetables; and wild mushrooms, berries, and herbs. It encourages the creative side of novice and seasoned cooks alike, prompting them to follow their instincts and "go wild" in the kitchen by adding, changing, or substituting ingredients in existing recipes. To help, a wealth of suggestions is found throughout. Beautiful illustrations and a list of organic foods sources complete this user-friendly cookbook.

Going Wild in the Kitchen is both a unique cookbook and a recipe for inspiration. So let yourself go! Excite your palate with this treasure-trove of unique, healthy, and taste-tempting recipe creations.

$16.95 • 240 pages • 7.5 x 9-inch quality paperback • ISBN 0-7570-0091-6

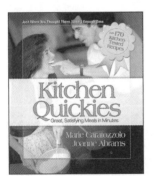

KITCHEN QUICKIES
Great, Satisfying Meals in Minutes
Marie Caratozzolo and Joanne Abrams

Ever feel that there aren't enough hours in the day to enjoy life's pleasures? Whether you're dealing with problems on the job, chasing after kids on the home front, or simply running from errand to errand, the evening probably finds you longing for a great meal, but without the time to prepare one.

Kitchen Quickies offers a solution. Virtually all of its over 170 kitchen-tested recipes—yes, really kitchen tested—call for a maximum of only five main ingredients other than kitchen staples, and each dish takes just minutes to prepare! Imagine being able to whip up dishes like Southwestern Tortilla Pizzas, Super Salmon Burgers, and Tuscan-Style Fusilli—in no time flat! As a bonus, these delicious dishes are actually good for you—low in fat and high in nutrients!

So the next time you think that there's simply no time to cook a great meal, pick up *Kitchen Quickies*. Who knows? You may even have time for a few "quickies" of your own.

$14.95 • 240 pages • 7.5 x 9-inch quality paperback • ISBN 0-7570-0085-1

THE MASON JAR COOKIE COOKBOOK
How to Create Mason Jar Cookie Mixes
Lonnette Parks

Nothing gladdens the heart like the tantalizing aroma of cookies baking in the oven. But for so many people, a busy lifestyle has made it impossible to find the time to bake at home—until now. Lonnette Parks, cookie baker extraordinaire, has not only developed fifty kitchen-tested recipes for delicious cookies, but has found a way for you to give the gift of home baking to everyone on your gift list.

For each mouth-watering cookie, the author provides the full recipe so that you can bake a variety of delights at home. In addition, she presents complete instructions for beautifully arranging the nonperishable ingredients in a Mason jar so that you can give the jar to a friend. By adding just a few common ingredients, your friend can then prepare fabulous home-baked cookies in a matter of minutes. Recipes include Best Ever Chocolate Chip Cookies, Blondies, and much, much more.

Whether you want to bake scrumptious cookies in your own kitchen or you'd like to give distinctive Mason jar cookie mixes to cookie-loving friends and family, *The Mason Jar Cookie Cookbook* is the perfect book.

$12.95 • 144 pages • 7.5 x 7.5-inch quality paperback • ISBN 0-7570-0046-0

THE MASON JAR SOUP-TO-NUTS COOKBOOK
How to Create Mason Jar Recipe Mixes
Lonnette Parks

In this follow-up to her best-selling book, *The Mason Jar Cookie Cookbook*, author and cook Lonnette Parks presents recipes for over fifty delicious soups, muffins, breads, cakes, pancakes, beverages, and more. And, just as in her previous book, the author tells you how to give the gift of home cooking to friends and family.

For each Mason jar creation, the author provides the full recipe so that you can cook and bake a variety of delights at home. In addition, she includes complete instructions for beautifully arranging the nonperishable ingredients in a Mason jar so that you can give the jar to a friend. Recipes include Golden Corn Bread, Double Chocolate Biscotti, Ginger Muffins, Apple Cinnamon Pancakes, Barley Rice Soup, Viennese Coffee, and much, much more.

$12.95 • 144 pages • 7.5 x 7.5-inch quality paperback • ISBN 0-7570-0129-7

THE COMPLETE MUFFIN COOKBOOK
The Ultimate Guide to Making Great Muffins

Gloria Ambrosia

Muffins aren't just for breakfast anymore! With the right combination of ingredients—think Swiss cheese, Dijon mustard, and tarragon—muffins are superb accompaniments to soups and salads, make a delicious snack, and are even welcome guests at the dinner table.

The Complete Muffin Cookbook is an extraordinary collection of delectable muffins that are made with wholesome, nutritious ingredients. There's even a chapter on "Low-Fat-and-Still-Yummy" creations. Best of all, author and muffin-baker Gloria Ambrosia generously shares her muffin-making wisdom. Her list of staples, detailing the various types of flour, sweeteners, and utensils used, help make sure her muffins are not only sensational, but also quick and easy to prepare. She also reveals the tips and techniques she has gathered over the years—from blending the ingredients to freezing the baked masterpieces for later enjoyment. From start to finish, you can whip up a tasty batch in less than thirty minutes.

So get ready to treat yourself to Gloria's exquisite array of muffins. Delicious, natural, immensely satisfying, and wonderfully simple to prepare, these taste-tempting delights can make any time of the day special.

$14.95 • 224 pages • 7.5 x 7.5-inch quality paperback • ISBN 0-7570-0179-3

**For more information about our books,
visit our website at www.squareonepublishers.com**